# AS/A-LEVEL YEAR 1

## STUDENT GUIDE

# OCR

# Psychology

## Component 1

### Research methods

Fiona Lintern

PHILIP ALLAN FOR
HODDER
EDUCATION
AN HACHETTE UK COMPANY

Philip Allan, an imprint of Hodder Education, an Hachette UK company, Blenheim Court, George Street, Banbury, Oxfordshire OX16 5BH

**Orders**

Bookpoint Ltd, 130 Milton Park, Abingdon, Oxfordshire OX14 4SB

tel: 01235 827827

fax: 01235 400401

e-mail: education@bookpoint.co.uk

Lines are open 9.00 a.m.–5.00 p.m., Monday to Saturday, with a 24-hour message answering service. You can also order through the Hodder Education website: www.hoddereducation.co.uk

© Fiona Lintern 2015

ISBN 978-1-4718-4413-3

First printed 2015

Impression number 5 4 3 2 1

Year 2019 2018 2017 2016 2015

This Guide has been written specifically to support students preparing for the OCR AS and A-level Psychology examinations. The content has been neither approved nor endorsed by OCR and remains the sole responsibility of the author.

Typeset by Integra Software Services Pvt. Ltd., Pondicherry, India

Cover photo: agsandrew/Fotolia

Printed in Italy

Hachette UK's policy is to use papers that are natural, renewable and recyclable products and made from wood grown in sustainable forests. The logging and manufacturing processes are expected to conform to the environmental regulations of the country of origin.

# Contents

## Content Guidance

## Questions & Answers

### Section A

### Section B

### Section C

# ■ Getting the most from this book

## Exam tips

Advice on key points in the text to help you learn and recall content, avoid pitfalls, and polish your exam technique in order to boost your grade.

## Knowledge check

Rapid-fire questions throughout the Content Guidance section to check your understanding.

## Knowledge check answers

1 Turn to the back of the book for the Knowledge check answers.

## Summaries

■ Each core topic is rounded off by a bullet-list summary for quick-check reference of what you need to know.

Exam-style questions

Commentary on the questions

Tips on what you need to do to gain full marks, indicated by the icon **e**

Sample student answers

Practise the questions, then look at the student answers that follow.

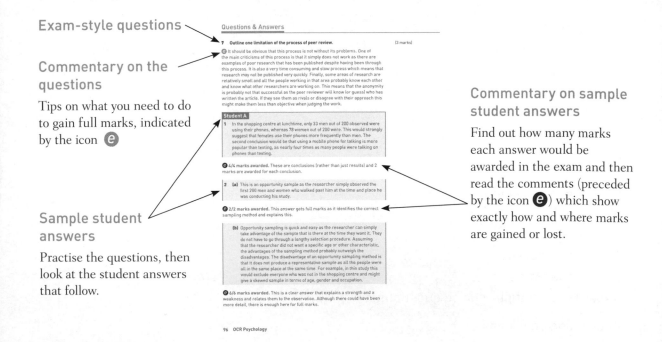

Commentary on sample student answers

Find out how many marks each answer would be awarded in the exam and then read the comments (preceded by the icon **e**) which show exactly how and where marks are gained or lost.

# ■ About this book

This book is a guide to **Component 1: Research methods** of the OCR AS and A-level psychology specifications. It is intended as a revision aid rather than as a textbook. Its purpose is to summarise the content, to explain how the content will be assessed, to look at the type of questions to expect and to consider sample answers.

There are two sections:

- **Content Guidance.** This takes you through the material that you need to cover for Component 1: Research methods of the AS and A-level examinations. There are sub-sections on the different methods with which you need to be familiar, along with advice on planning research, recording and analysing data and report writing. This is followed by guidance on the different tasks that might be set in the examination: evaluating research, dealing with data and designing research.
- **Questions & Answers.** This section provides sample questions and answers that are followed by a commentary and marks. Look at the responses and commentary and try to apply the best techniques to your own answers.

## Getting started

You will need a file (or folder) and some dividers. There are six sections in the specification for this component so you could start by dividing your file into six sections. You should also include a section into which you can put all your assessed work (do not throw it away — keep it and revise from it, rewriting any answers that did not get full marks). You are also advised to take every opportunity to conduct your own psychological research. You will learn a great deal from this and it would be advisable to keep all this material together.

## The specification

Component 1: Research methods examines your knowledge and understanding of research methods. Although you are not examined specifically on the research activities that you have conducted, it is advisable to carry out as much practical research as you can. This will not only allow you to become familiar with each of the data-collecting techniques, but will also give you first-hand experience of many of the evaluative issues that this book covers.

There will be three sections in the AS and A-level examinations. Section A will consist of multiple-choice questions; section B is research design and response and asks you to respond to a piece of source material; section C focuses on data analysis and interpretation, again in response to a piece of source material. These sections appear on both the AS and the A-level examination papers, although the mark allocations differ between the two papers.

On both the AS and the A-level examination paper 10% of the marks available will be for assessment of mathematics skills within the context of psychology. These skills will be at a Level 2 (GCSE level) or higher standard. The specification states that any lower level mathematical skills may still be assessed within examination papers but will not count within the 10% weighting for psychology. Further guidance on this is given in the Questions & Answers section of this guide.

# Content Guidance

## ■ Research methods and techniques

### Experiment

Psychologists use experiments to test their ideas. There are several kinds of experiments but they all attempt to measure the effect of one variable on another. Here laboratory experiments, field experiments and natural/quasi experiments will be examined.

### Laboratory experiments

A laboratory experiment is an experiment conducted in a controlled situation. The researcher will manipulate one variable (the **independent variable** or **IV**) and measure its effect on another variable (the **dependent variable** or **DV**). For example, if you thought that the amount of light in a room affected the amount of work that students did, you could test this experimentally by varying the amount of light that was in the room and measuring the amount of work that was done. There are a number of different experimental designs that could be used to do this and this is covered on pages 18 and 19.

---

### Evaluation

#### Strengths
- Manipulation of independent variables can indicate cause-and-effect relationships
- Increased control and accurate measurement
- Standardised procedures mean that replication is possible

#### Weaknesses
- Artificial conditions may produce unnatural behaviour, which means that the research lacks ecological validity
- Results may be biased by sampling, demand characteristics and/or experimenter bias
- Total control over all variables is never possible
- There may be ethical problems of deception etc.

---

### Exam tip

For any experiment, make sure that you know which is the independent variable and which is the dependent variable. The independent variable is always the one being manipulated and the dependent variable is the one being measured. This is covered in more detail on pages 13 and 20.

# Field experiments

Field experiments are carried out in a natural environment, but the independent variable is still manipulated by the experimenter.

## Evaluation

### Strengths
- Greater ecological validity because surroundings are natural
- Less likelihood of demand characteristics (if people are unaware of the research taking place)

### Weaknesses
- Difficulties in controlling the situation, therefore more possibility of bias from extraneous variables
- Difficult to replicate
- Time-consuming
- Ethical problems of consent, deception, invasion of privacy etc.

# Natural (or quasi) experiments

Natural experiments take place in circumstances that allow the researcher to examine the effect of a naturally occurring independent variable. Natural experiments are often used where artificial manipulation of a variable would be impossible or unethical. For example, it is not possible to manipulate artificially age or sex for experimental reasons, so an experiment comparing different age groups or comparing the performance of males and females would be a natural experiment.

## Evaluation

### Strengths
- Greater ecological validity since the change in the independent variable is a natural one
- Allows researchers to investigate areas that would otherwise be unavailable to them
- Increased validity of findings due to lack of experimenter manipulation
- If subjects are unaware of being studied, there will be little bias from demand characteristics

### Weaknesses
- Difficult to infer cause and effect due to lack of control over extraneous variables and no manipulation of independent variable
- Impossible to replicate exactly
- May be subject to bias if participants know that they are being studied
- Ethical problems of consent, deception, invasion of privacy etc.

**Exam tip**

A 'field' in this sense means testing people in their natural environments rather than in an artificial laboratory environment.

**Knowledge check 1**

Identify one Core Study that was conducted in the 'field' (a natural environment) rather than in a laboratory. What are the strengths and weaknesses of using this method?

# Observation

In an observation, the researcher will simply observe without manipulation and attempt to record the behaviour that he or she observes. The fact that there is no manipulation makes this a non-experimental technique.

## Structured and unstructured observations

Although an observation can be conducted by simply trying to write down everything that is observed (this would be termed an **unstructured observation**), it is more usual to develop a coding scheme or set of categories that can simply be ticked when the appropriate behaviours are seen. This sort of observation can be referred to as a **structured observation**.

## Controlled and naturalistic observations

Observations can be conducted within laboratory settings (**controlled observation**) or in more natural environments (**naturalistic observations**). In a controlled observation it is much more likely that the participants will be aware of being observed as they are likely to be in an artificial setting. In the same way that laboratory experiments have high levels of control and lower levels of realism compared to naturalistic observations, we can say that controlled observations have higher control than naturalistic observations and lower levels of realism.

## Participant and non-participant observation

Generally an observation is conducted with the observer remaining 'outside' the situation that he or she is observing. This is termed **non-participant observation**. An alternative is to conduct **participant observation**, where the researcher becomes a part of the group that is being observed, perhaps by getting a job in a factory in order to conduct his or her observation of work practices.

## Overt and covert observations

Observations can also be covert or overt. A **covert observation** is where the people being observed are unaware of being observed and an **overt observation** is where the people being observed are aware of the observation taking place.

---

### Evaluation

**Strengths**

- High ecological validity, where 'real' behaviour is being observed — especially where people are unaware of being observed
- Can produce extremely 'rich' data
- Low demand characteristics, where people are unaware of being observed
- Can be used where it would be difficult or unethical to manipulate variables
- Can be used to generate hypotheses for further experimental research

## Weaknesses

- Lack of control over variables, as nothing is being manipulated/held constant
- Difficult to conclude cause-and-effect relationships, as no variables are being manipulated
- Can be subject to observer bias
- Can be difficult to ensure inter-rater reliability
- Extremely difficult to replicate
- Ethical issues if people are observed without their permission
- Problems of demand characteristics if people are observed with their permission

# Self-report

## Questionnaires and interviews

Self-report methods are techniques for asking people directly for information. This might be done by conducting interviews or questionnaires. **Questionnaires** may be completed by the participants or may consist of a set of questions that the researcher reads to the participant, whose answers are then recorded. **Interviews** may be structured so that every participant receives exactly the same question(s), or may be semi-structured so that the researcher has some standard questions but is able to respond to the participant by asking additional questions or exploring interesting issues that arise from the answers.

## Evaluation

### Strengths

- Asking people directly, rather than trying to work out reasons for their behaviour from other methods, such as observation
- Large amounts of data can be collected relatively quickly and cheaply, which can increase representativeness and generalisability
- Replicable
- Closed questions are easy to score/analyse

### Weaknesses

- People may give answers based on social desirability bias, acquiescence or response set
- Questions/scales may be interpreted differently by participants
- Closed questions may force people into choosing answers that do not reflect their true opinion
- Open questions are extremely difficult to score/analyse

---

**Exam tip**

Note that observation can also be used as a technique for collecting data within an experiment. For example, in a study of the effects of observing television violence, children might be exposed to different degrees of violence (keeping ethical considerations in mind of course), then their levels of aggression could be measured using an observation. This would still be an experiment.

**Knowledge check 3**

Identify a Core Study that used observational techniques. Remember that some studies may use observation as a way of collecting data within an experiment.

**Exam tip**

Think about the Core Studies that you have covered. Which ones use self-report methods?

**Knowledge check 4**

Outline at least two strengths and two weaknesses of self-report methods.

# Correlation

Strictly speaking, correlation is a method of statistical analysis rather than a research method. A correlation shows a relationship between two variables. No manipulation takes place and both variables are measured. Results are generally plotted on a scatter graph that displays the direction and strength of the relationship.

A **positive correlation** between two variables means that as the scores on one variable increase, so do the scores on the other variable (see Figure 1). However, this does not mean that the increase in one variable *causes* the increase on the other variable; it simply means that the two variables are positively related.

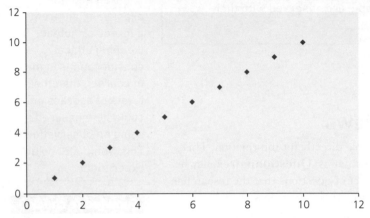

**Figure 1** A perfect positive correlation

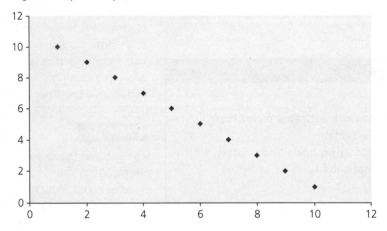

**Figure 2** A perfect negative correlation

**Exam tip**

It is important that you understand that correlation only shows a relationship between two variables rather than showing that a change in one variable causes a change in the other variable.

A **negative correlation** between two variables means that as the scores on one variable increase, the scores on the other variable decrease (see Figure 2). Again, this does not show cause and effect, but simply that the variables are negatively related.

Imagine that a teacher decided to find out the relationship between the number of hours of sleep that a student had on the previous night and the speed at which he or she can work. This is not an experiment, so the teacher does not need to manipulate anything. She would just need to decide how to measure each of these variables, and this means using whatever techniques she felt were most appropriate.

To measure the number of hours of sleep that a student has had the previous night, a self-report technique could be used and the student could simply be asked to give the information, for example in answer to the following question: 'How many hours of sleep did you get last night?'.

This looks like a straightforward question and is certainly a simple technique for getting the data. However, it might be that the participants do not actually know the answer to this question and they may simply guess. It might also be that they think the teacher is asking them because of an ulterior motive, so they may say that they had 8 hours of sleep in order to avoid being told off for not getting enough sleep on a school night. They may also say that they only had 3 hours of sleep because they are being asked in front of the rest of the class and they think that this answer would impress their friends.

> **Exam tip**
>
> Because correlation is a method of analysing relationships, any study using this technique may be affected by the strengths and weaknesses associated with the choice of measurement.

So what can we conclude from this research? Suppose that the teacher finds that the students who had the most sleep completed the jigsaw the fastest. This does not mean that she can infer that getting a good night's sleep causes an improvement in the speed of work. All she has shown is that there is a relationship between the two variables. There may be a third variable that explains this relationship (such as dedicated students working harder and not going out late as much), or the relationship may simply be coincidence. However, the results of this correlation could be used to generate ideas for further experimental research that might demonstrate that participants who were allowed 8 hours of sleep completed a task faster than participants who were only allowed 5 hours of sleep.

> **Knowledge check 5**
>
> The teacher decides to use the speed at which students can complete a jigsaw puzzle as her measure of 'speed of work'. Suggest one weakness this choice of measurement may have, and then propose two other ways in which 'speed of work' may be measured.

## Evaluation

### Strengths

- Gives precise information on the degree of relationship between variables
- No manipulation is required, so correlation can be used in situations where experimentation would be impossible or unethical
- In some cases, strong significant correlations can suggest ideas for experimental studies to determine cause-and-effect relationships

### Weaknesses

- No cause and effect can be inferred
- Technique is subject to any problems associated with the method used to collect data (e.g. self-report or observation may have been used to measure variables)

**Task**

Using the correlational technique, suggest how you might investigate the relationship between the amount of coffee that people drink and their stress levels. Explain clearly how you would measure each variable. To see whether you have understood, suggest which method would be the most appropriate for investigating the topics listed below. If you can think of more than one method that could be used, consider issues such as ethics, ecological validity, demand characteristics etc. to decide which you think would be most appropriate.

- study habits of sixth formers
- sleep habits of university students
- superstitious behaviour
- the effects of television violence on behaviour
- the effects of noise on memory
- the effect of audiences on sport performance
- attitudes to homeless people
- the relationship between time spent watching television and time spent doing homework
- mobile phone usage
- aggressive behaviour in the playground

**Knowledge check 6**

Assuming that you found a positive relationship between coffee intake and stress (as coffee intake increases, so do stress levels), does this mean that you have demonstrated that:

**A** drinking coffee makes people stressed?

**B** high stress levels make people drink more coffee?

**C** neither A nor B?

Explain your answer.

**Summary**

- The four methods that you need for the exam are experiments, observations, self-reports and correlations.
- Each method has strengths and weaknesses, which have been summarised for you in the evaluation boxes.

- One of the most important issues to consider is control: experiments tend to be higher in control than other methods as the experimenter is able to manipulate the variables. However, this may lead to a lack of ecological validity or realism.
- Other methods (such as observation) may be much higher in realism but at the expense of being able to control the environment.

# ■ Planning and conducting research

## Aims and hypotheses and how to formulate

## Research aims and research questions

Research always begins with questions. You can probably think of many questions about human behaviour. Some of these might be quite general, for example just wondering how noise influences learning or how competition affects sports performance.

Research aims are precise statements of what the research aims to investigate. For example the research question 'How does noise affect learning?' could become a research aim to 'investigate the effect of background noise on the learning of word lists' and the research question 'How does competition affect sports performance?' could become an aim to 'investigate the effect of competition on the number of press-ups someone can complete'.

# Hypotheses

Once you have identified a research question and then a more focused research aim, you will need to construct (or 'frame') a hypothesis. A hypothesis is a testable statement. It establishes what you think the relationship between two variables is.

For an experiment, the **alternative hypothesis** (sometimes called the experimental hypothesis) would state how one variable (the independent variable, or IV) is likely to affect another variable (the dependent variable, or DV). If you are asked to write a hypothesis in the examination, you need to think carefully about the appropriate wording.

The following are examples of clearly worded hypotheses:

- Participants will remember more words from a list of 20 nouns when learning takes place in a quiet environment than when learning takes place in a noisy environment.
- Participants will complete more press-ups in 2 minutes when in competition with another person than when alone.

These are clear statements: we know exactly what each variable is and how the independent variable will affect the dependent variable. These are also **one-tailed hypotheses**, which mean that the direction of the effect has been predicted: the researchers have predicted that people will remember *more* words and complete *more* press-ups.

It is not essential to predict the direction of the effect. If you conducted an experiment where you were unable to decide how you thought the independent variable might affect the dependent variable, you would produce a **two-tailed hypothesis**. This would be worded as follows:

- The noise level in a room will affect how many words people remember from a list of 20 nouns.
- Competition will affect the number of press-ups that a person can complete in 2 minutes.

You could also be asked to write a **null hypothesis**. This is the 'no effect' hypothesis and is the other possible outcome to your research: either the independent variable will affect the dependent variable in the way that you predict, or it will not. Conducting statistical analysis on your data would allow you to decide which of these statements is accepted and which is rejected (see page 33 for more guidance on statistical analysis).

Null hypotheses would be worded as follows:

- The noise level in a room will not affect how many words people remember from a list of 20 nouns **OR** There will be no difference in the number of words participants remember from a list of 20 nouns when learning takes place in a quiet environment compared to a noisy environment.

**Exam tip**

Make sure you understand the difference between a research aim and a research question by trying to identify both in the Core Studies that you are covering.

**Exam tip**

Practise writing hypotheses for some of the Core Studies. Make sure you can identify the IV and the DV for each one.

- Competition will not affect the number of press-ups that a person can complete in 2 minutes **OR** There will be no difference in the number of press-ups participants can complete in 2 minutes when in competition with another person compared to alone.

Remember that a null hypothesis is not the opposite of the alternate hypothesis. It is not correct to predict 'more words' or 'more press-ups' in the experimental hypothesis and then to change this to 'fewer words' or 'fewer press-ups' in the null hypothesis — this is still predicting that the independent variable is going to have an effect on the dependent variable. The null hypothesis must predict no effect.

If the research is correlational rather than experimental, both hypotheses need to be worded appropriately. Rather than predicting an *effect*, you are now predicting a *relationship*. An alternative hypothesis for a correlation might be: 'There will be a positive relationship between the number of hours of sleep a participant has had and his or her score on a word-search task.' The null would be: 'There will be no relationship between the number of hours of sleep a participant has had and his or her score on a word-search task.'

To check your understanding, complete the following tasks.

### Task 1

For each of the following hypotheses, decide whether it is alternate or null:

- There will be no difference in the time taken to complete a jigsaw in the morning and in the evening.
- People will complete a jigsaw puzzle faster after drinking coffee than after drinking a non-caffeinated drink.
- There is no difference between the memory scores of males and females.
- Age will not affect performance on a mathematics test.
- There will be a positive relationship between age and ability to solve anagrams.
- There will be a negative relationship between age and ability to solve anagrams.

### Task 2

Identify the IV and the DV in each of the following hypotheses:

- Age will not affect performance on a mathematics test.
- People will complete more press-ups in 2 minutes when in competition than when working alone.
- Males will complete a football-related word search faster than females.
- Eating breakfast improves performance on a reaction-time task.
- Participants will achieve a higher score on a memory test when working in a warm room than in a cold room.

> **Exam tip**
>
> This is important as students often write the opposite of their hypothesis when asked for a null hypothesis. Make sure that you write a 'no-effect' hypothesis if you are asked to write a null hypothesis.

**Task 3**

Write appropriate hypotheses for the following experiments:
- the effect of music on memory
- the effect of age on reaction time
- the effect of time of day on puzzle-solving speed

**Task 4**

Write appropriate hypotheses for the following correlations:
- the relationship between extraversion and time spent watching television
- the relationship between temperature and aggression
- the relationship between coffee intake and stress

**Exam tip**

You are likely to be asked to write hypotheses (note the plural, meaning hypothesis and null hypothesis) in the examination. The more you practise writing them, the easier this will get.

## Summary

- Hypotheses are testable statements.
- An alternate hypothesis predicts that the independent variable will have an effect on the dependent variable and a null hypothesis predicts that there will be no effect.

- A one-tailed hypothesis predicts the direction of the effect and a two-tailed hypothesis simply predicts an effect without specifying the direction of this effect.

# Populations, samples and sampling techniques

One of the crucial issues when conducting psychological research is the choice of participants. The key concepts to consider here are the extent to which your sample of participants is representative of a larger population and the extent to which you are able to generalise your findings to a larger population. These are obviously linked: a representative sample will allow you to generalise more easily than an unrepresentative sample.

The terms '**population**' or '**target population**' are used to describe the whole group of people in whom the researcher is interested. The term '**sample**' refers to the group of people that are selected to take part in the research.

# Different sampling methods

## Random sampling

A random sample is a sample that has been selected in a way that means everyone in the target population has an equal opportunity of being chosen. This is equivalent to putting the names of everyone in the target population in a hat and drawing out the number of names that you require. Usually, the selection procedure is done on computer using random number generators. Everyone in the target population is given a number, then a computer programme generates a random selection of numbers and the corresponding people are selected.

**Knowledge check 7**

Think about the Core Study conducted by Milgram. Identify the target population *and* the sample for this study.

**Exam tip**

Make sure that you understand both terms in the above question and that you answer both parts of such a question.

> **Evaluation**
>
> **Strengths**
> - Everyone in the target population has an equal chance of being selected
> - Sample is (should be!) representative of target population
>
> **Weaknesses**
> - More complex and time-consuming than other methods (especially opportunity sampling)
> - Can be difficult (or even impossible) if the target population is large and the researcher does not have names etc.

## Opportunity sampling

An opportunity sample is one that is selected by 'opportunity' or convenience: the researcher simply uses the people that are present at the time that he or she is conducting the research. This is a popular method for student research, although there are obvious weaknesses with this way of selecting a sample.

> **Evaluation**
>
> **Strengths**
> - Quick and easy to select the sample as you simply take advantage of the people that are around you when you conduct your research
> - No need to select people because of predetermined categories or characteristics
>
> **Weaknesses**
> - May be biased as unlikely to be representative of a target population

## Snowball sampling

A snowball sample is another convenience sample. Snowball sampling is a technique where each participant is asked to suggest another potential participant and so the whole sample is built up a little like a snowball rolling down a hill. Snowball sampling is typically used when members of the target population might be difficult to identify. For example, in a study of any very uncommon behaviours or experiences, it might be an effective strategy to ask each participant to suggest someone else.

> **Evaluation**
>
> **Strengths**
> - May be effective in targeting difficult to identify participants
> - Can target/request participants who may possess the features under investigation
>
> **Weaknesses**
> - Can be slow
> - May not be representative of a target population

# Self-selected sampling

A self-selected sample is one where people volunteer to take part in a research project.

## Evaluation

### Strengths
- May be a relatively easy way of achieving a sample
- Can target/request participants who may possess the features under investigation

### Weaknesses
- Unlikely to be representative of a larger population

### Exam tip

Make sure that you understand the difference between these sampling techniques. A random sample is not the same as an opportunity sample, so avoid using the phrase 'randomly selected' unless you mean using a random sampling technique.

### Task

Which sampling method has been used in the following studies?

1 A student selected his sample by going to the sixth-form common room and asking the first 20 people he saw to complete a questionnaire.

2 A researcher put the names of everyone in a school in a hat and drew out 50 names.

3 A researcher went to a shopping centre and asked the first 30 people she saw to answer some questions.

4 A researcher put up a poster asking anyone who was interested in taking part in research to come to the psychology department on Monday afternoon.

5 Every address in a town is given a number and then a random number generator is used to generate 100 numbers. The corresponding addresses are selected as the sample.

6 A researcher wishes to interview homeless people. He identifies three participants through a shelter and asks them to suggest other potential participants.

7 A researcher advertises for participants in a newspaper.

### Knowledge check 8

Using issues relating to sample and sampling methods, outline one weakness with each of the following studies:
- a study on attitudes to sixth-form life that selected an opportunity sample from the sixth-form quiet study room during lunchtime
- a survey of helping behaviour where all the respondents are volunteers

## Summary

- It is obviously very important in any piece of research that we have a sample that will allow us to generalise our findings beyond this sample.

- However, we must always be careful not to generalise our findings too far and claim that results gained from one very small local sample can be applied to groups of very different people.

# Experimental designs

We have already looked at a number of different methods in the previous section. If we have chosen to use an experiment to investigate our hypothesis, there are a number of different experimental designs that could be used to do this. The most important experimental designs are the independent measures design, the repeated measures design and the matched pairs design.

> ### Exam tip
>
> A laboratory experiment is conducted in a controlled situation. The researcher will manipulate one variable (the **independent variable** or **IV**) and measure its effect on another variable (the **dependent variable** or **DV**). For example, if you thought that the amount of light in a room affected the amount of work that students did, you could test this experimentally by varying the amount of light that was in the room and measuring the amount of work that was done.

## Independent measures design

An independent measures design is one that uses two (or more) conditions, with different participants in each condition. To use an independent measures design for the 'light and work' experiment mentioned in the exam tip, you would test one group of participants in a well-lit room and another group in a poorly-lit room. You could give the participants the same task to do and then compare how much each group has completed.

### Evaluation

#### Strengths
- Participants only have to do the task once so they are less likely to get bored or to work out what it is that is being tested (which may affect how they behave)
- The same task can be used with each group

#### Weaknesses
- As there are different participants in each group, there may be differences between them, which means that it is possible that the difference between them is what produced the difference in results (rather than the difference between the two conditions)

## Repeated measures design

A repeated measures design is one that uses the same participants in each condition. This time, you would need to test the participants in a well-lit room and then test them again in a poorly-lit room. You could then compare the results for each condition.

### Knowledge check 9

What is the independent variable in the experiment described here?

### Knowledge check 10

There are advantages and disadvantages to each of these experimental designs. Try to identify the strengths and weaknesses of using an independent measures design to investigate the effect of the amount of light on the amount of work completed by students.

### Knowledge check 11

Identify the strengths and weaknesses of using a repeated measures design to investigate the effect of the amount of light on the amount of work completed by students.

## Evaluation

### Strengths

- The participants are the same in each group, so it is easier to compare their performance in each condition
- You need fewer participants as they will take part in each condition

### Weaknesses

- Either the participants will do the same task twice, which may lead to boredom or improvement and may help them work out what is being tested, or you will need two different tasks, which may make comparisons more difficult as one task may be easier than the other

There is a third design that can be used that may overcome some of the problems described above.

# Matched pairs design

A matched pairs design is one where different participants are used in each condition but the researcher attempts to make the two groups of participants as similar as possible. This could be done by measuring the participants' ability on some appropriate measure beforehand and then pairing those who have a similar level of ability. One of each pair is then allocated to each condition.

## Evaluation

### Strengths

- Participants only have to be tested once
- Differences between the two groups have been reduced

### Weaknesses

- A lengthy and time-consuming process that can be quite 'wasteful' of participants as a large number of people would need to be tested to find appropriate pairs

**Exam tip**

There are always strengths and weaknesses for whichever design you choose. The important thing is that you are able to discuss them fully.

**Exam tip**

You could be asked to decide which design would be most appropriate for a specific experiment. For example, for the experiment described here, decide which design you think would be most appropriate and give your reasons.

**Exam tip**

Think about the Core Studies you have covered. Make sure you can identify the experimental designs discussed here.

## Summary

- Each design has its own strengths and weaknesses and researchers often have to choose a design for a study where the strengths outweigh the weaknesses rather than one that has no weaknesses at all.

- It is a useful evaluative skill to be able to consider whether a different design could be used in a particular study and the effect that this might have.

# Operationalising and measuring variables

Most research ideas start out by being quite general. For example, you might want to design an experiment looking at some of the factors that influence memory, generating the following ideas (possible **independent variables**):

- time of day
- hunger
- room temperature
- stress
- motivation
- competition
- presentation of material — font size, colour etc.

Let us look at presentation of material and specifically font size. This is quite a simple way to operationalise a variable. We now know the specific variable that will be manipulated, so we decide to give one group of participants material to learn that has been printed in font size 10 and the other groups the same material in font size 12. We now have the two conditions of our experiment.

It is important that we only vary one aspect of the presentation of material at a time. In this experiment, we have decided to vary the font size. Everything else must be kept constant (**control**): the participants in each group will see the material printed in the same font and the same colour, the only change being to the font size.

> ### Exam tip
>
> If we were to vary more than one feature, we would have difficulties drawing conclusions from our research. For example, if one group had material printed in Times New Roman font size 10 and the other group in Arial font size 12, we would not be able to decide whether it was the font style or the font size that was responsible for any differences in memory.

Now we need to think about the **dependent variable**. The ways that memory could be measured (possible dependent variables) include:

- recall from word list
- recognition from word list
- test on content of text

If we decide to use the last suggestion, we would need to find an appropriate text to present in different font sizes and then design a series of questions to test the participants' recall of their text. This might give us 'number of facts recalled' as our dependent variable.

We now have an operationalised alternative hypothesis: 'People will recall more facts from a text presented in font size 12 than from one presented in front size 10.'

The null hypothesis would be: 'There will be no difference in the number of facts recalled from a text presented in font size 12 compared to a text presented in font size 10' or 'Font size will have no effect on recall of facts'.

To check your understanding, try the following activity.

> ### Knowledge check 12
>
> Suggest how the variable 'naughtiness in children' could be operationalised.

**Task**

You have been asked to conduct an experiment to investigate the effect of time of day on learning. Propose three different ways in which this experiment could be conducted. For each suggestion:

- identify the design that you would use
- explain how the IV could be operationalised
- suggest how the DV could be measured

Now consider the strengths and weaknesses of each of your suggestions. Which do you think would be the most valid test of the effect of time of day on learning?

# Control of extraneous variables

If we are conducting experimental research, we will attempt to control as many variables as possible so that we can be sure that any changes in the dependent variable are due to the manipulation of the independent variable and not to any other variable. If there are uncontrolled variables (and it is virtually impossible to control for everything), these are referred to as extraneous or potential confounding variables. For example, if we were to conduct an experiment into the effects of the amount of light on the speed at which participants could conduct a task but we conducted the first condition in the morning and the second condition in the afternoon, we would not be sure if the change in speed was due to the amount of light or the time of day (or even something else such as level of hunger).

**Exam tip**

Write your own definition of an extraneous variable.

**Knowledge check 13**

Identify one extraneous (potential confounding) variable in the study by Loftus and Palmer.

**Summary**

- You might still be finding all the terms and concepts of hypotheses and variables a little bit confusing but don't worry. It is all about being precise when you conduct research.

- A hypothesis needs to state *exactly* what you expect to happen and the more clearly defined (operationalised) your variables are, the easier it will be to identify the conditions of your independent variable and to design ways of measuring your dependent variable.

# Designing observations

## Behavioural categories

If you are going to conduct an observation, you will need a very clear idea of what you are going to observe. You could do this by using **behavioural categories**. For example, if you were observing children in a classroom your behavioural categories might be working on computer, reading, discussing something with another child and so on. If you were observing adults interacting in a business meeting, your behavioural categories might be asking questions, making suggestions, answering other people's questions and so on. Having clear behavioural categories before you begin your observation will make the process of recording your observations much easier. Designing a grid or coding sheet to record the data on will also help.

# Coding frames

Coding frames are another way to ensure that you are categorising and recording behaviour systematically. A coding frame consists of a number of pre-determined codes (abbreviations or symbols for example) that attempt to cover all of the behaviours that you might see. In the example above where the observation is taking place in a classroom your coding frame might include the following:

- CW = computer work
- RD = reading
- DIS = discussing

And in the example relating to a business meeting your coding frame might include:

- ASKQ = asking questions
- ANSQ = answering questions
- SUG = making suggestions

Having clear behavioural categories and a coding frame established before you start will make the process of collecting and recording data much easier than if you were trying to write down everything that was happening. The use of behavioural categories and coding frames also helps with inter-rater reliability (see page 36).

(see page 36)

> **Exam tip**
>
> If you are asked to design an observation in the examination, make sure that you include clear behavioural categories and a simple coding frame.

# Sampling techniques

Observations can be carried out using the following techniques:

- **Time sampling**, where the researcher observes everything that occurs within a certain time period. For example, recording behaviour in a classroom could be done by observing each child for 1 minute and recording what he or she is doing, then moving on to the next child. Recording mother–infant interactions could be done by coding the behaviour at 30-second intervals.
- **Event sampling**, where the researcher records a specific event every time it occurs. For example, recording behaviour in a classroom could be done by producing a list of all possible behaviours (perhaps by conducting a pilot study) and then ticking the appropriate box every time the behaviour is observed.

> **Exam tip**
>
> Make sure you know the difference between these types of sampling.

> **Task**
>
> You have been asked to conduct an observation to find out exactly what sixth form students use their study room for. Suggest the categories that you could use for this observation, then outline some of the problems that you might encounter if you were to conduct this observation.

# Inter-rater reliability

If observations are conducted by more than one observer, it is important to consider the issue of **inter-rater reliability**. This is the extent to which observers agree on the way that behaviours should be categorised. High inter-rater reliability means that the observers are in close agreement. High levels of inter-rate reliability can be achieved through training observers and making categories clear and unambiguous.

> **Knowledge check 14**
>
> Why is inter-rater reliability so important?

## Summary

- It is important that you know exactly how you are going to conduct your observation.

- Constructing behavioural categories or a coding frame will help you collect data accurately and objectively.

# Designing self-reports

There are many different ways that you can ask questions. A simple distinction is between open questions and closed questions. **Open questions** are simply questions that ask the participant to give a response in his or her own words. An example of an open question would be 'What do you think of AS psychology?'

If you asked a number of people this question, you would probably get a variety of types of answers. Some people may simply say that they like it or that they do not like it, while others may give you lots of information. Although asking open questions will give you a fair amount of detail, it may be difficult to draw general conclusions from a group of people.

An alternative to this may be to ask **closed questions**, which require the participants to choose from a range of pre-determined answers. An example of a closed question would be 'Do you like AS psychology?' (the choice of answers being 'yes' or 'no' only). This would not give you as much information about what people actually think about AS psychology, but it would allow you to draw a general conclusion, for example that out of 20 people, 17 said that they liked AS psychology and three said that they did not.

You could get a little more from a closed question by asking it this way:

Tick the statement that best describes your feelings about AS psychology:

1  I like AS psychology a lot. ☐

2  I like AS psychology a little. ☐

3  I neither like nor dislike AS psychology. ☐

4  I dislike AS psychology a little. ☐

5  I dislike AS psychology a lot. ☐

This time, you may find that the questioning of the same 20 people produces the following results:
- 6 say that they like AS psychology a lot
- 11 say that they like AS psychology a little
- 1 says that he or she neither likes nor dislikes AS psychology
- 2 say that they dislike AS psychology a little
- 0 say that they dislike AS psychology a lot

This type of questioning provides you with more precise information. However, there may still be problems. For example, do you know that everyone you asked interpreted the phrases 'a little' or 'a lot' in the same way? Maybe someone who said that he or she liked AS psychology a lot actually has the same feelings as someone who said that he or she only liked it a little but has interpreted the words differently. In this case, perhaps the distinction between 'a little' and 'a lot' is too broad and there should be another category in between.

**Exam tip**

Practise writing open and closed questions on a range of topics.

An alternative to this would be to use a **rating scale** (sometimes referred to as a Likert scale). If you used a rating scale to ask the question, it would look like this:

> Using the scale below where 1 = I dislike AS psychology a lot and 10 = I like AS psychology a lot, choose the number that best reflects your feelings about AS psychology:
>
> 1    2    3    4    5    6    7    8    9    10

This would give you an even more detailed set of results. This time, you might have results similar to this:

| Ratings of AS Psychology where 1 = dislike a lot and 10 = like a lot | Number of people |
|---|---|
| 1 | 0 |
| 2 | 1 |
| 3 | 2 |
| 4 | 1 |
| 5 | 1 |
| 6 | 4 |
| 7 | 4 |
| 8 | 2 |
| 9 | 3 |
| 10 | 2 |

This type of questioning has produced a great deal of information about the participants' feelings about AS psychology. However, you still need to be cautious in interpreting this information. Would everyone interpret the numerical scale in the same way? Do the four people who chose number 6 all have exactly the same opinion about how much they like AS psychology? You should not assume that they do, and so you need to take care when drawing conclusions from these results.

## Semantic differential scales

Another way of measuring opinions or attitudes is to use a semantic differential scale. This is where participants are asked to rate the topic (e.g. feelings about AS psychology) using pairs of opposing adjectives (usually referred to as bipolar adjectives) on a seven-point scale.

For example:

Rate your opinion of your psychology course.

| | | |
|---|---|---|
| Not interesting | 1 2 3 4 5 6 7 | Very interesting |
| Not challenging | 1 2 3 4 5 6 7 | Very challenging |
| No fun | 1 2 3 4 5 6 7 | Lots of fun |

**Exam tip**

Make sure you know the strengths and weaknesses of the different types of questions.

## Task

- Design a questionnaire asking psychology students for their opinions of their psychology course. Your questionnaire should include a range of open and closed questions and at least one rating scale. Try to ask more than just how much they like the course.

- When you have finished your questionnaire, evaluate it. Are there any problems with any of the questions? What could you conclude from the results if you used this questionnaire? What would you need to be cautious about?

## Summary

- There are a range of techniques that can be used to investigate human behaviour. The more familiar you are with considering how a piece of research could be conducted the easier you will find the research design and response section in the examination.

- Each of these techniques has strengths and weaknesses and there is no such thing as a piece of research which has no limitations at all. It is about selecting the most appropriate technique for the question that you are investigating. Remember that psychologists might conduct a range of studies on the same topic, using a variety of different methods, so as to build up the most complete picture possible.

# Data recording, analysis and presentation

## Raw data

Raw data are the data that are collected from your participants, before any sort of analysis is conducted. In order to collect data accurately you might need to design and use a raw data recording table.

Imagine you were conducting a study to see if males completed a task faster or slower than females you could simply record the data in a list as follows:

- Participant 1 male 35 secs
- Participant 2 male 56 secs
- Participant 3 female 45 secs
- and so on

However, it would make much more sense to construct a data table as follows:

| Male | | Female | |
|---|---|---|---|
| Participant no. | Time | Participant no. | Time |
| 1 | 35 | 1 | 45 |
| 2 | 56 | 2 | |

**Exam tip**

For each piece of research that you have conducted, think about the raw data that you collected. Did you design a table to record these data? Can you think of any improvements that you could make to these tables?

A table like this would keep your data organised and would make it far less likely that you would make any mistakes. It would also make it much easier to work out averages when you are ready to start analysing your data.

## Levels and types of data

Raw data come in a variety of forms. The types of data that you are likely to come across in psychology are as follows:

- **Nominal data.** This is when data are simply put into categories or when frequencies are being counted. These are the simplest form of data.
- **Ordinal data.** These are data that have been put into rank order: first, second, third etc. Ordinal data give us more information than nominal data but are still limited because we do not know how large the gap is between the first and second place or between the second and third place. We do not know whether these gaps are the same for each.
- **Interval (and ratio) data.** These are data on an objective scale with equal intervals, for example, time, temperature or length. Ratio data are similar to interval data but have the added property of having an absolute zero point and no minus numbers. You are unlikely to have to distinguish between interval and ratio data.

## Quantitative and qualitative data

The simplest distinction between these types of data is that quantitative data are data in numbers and qualitative data are data in words.

For example, if a researcher collected opinions on student attitudes to their psychology course by asking them to rate aspects of the course such as interest, enjoyment and challenge on 1–10 scales these would be quantitative data. If the researcher asked students to write (or speak) about their opinions of the course these would be qualitative data.

### Evaluation: quantitative data

**Strengths**
- Easy to analyse
- Can summarise large amounts of data
- Some behaviours can be quantified

**Weaknesses**
- Some behaviours cannot be easily quantified and collecting only quantitative data may mean that researchers miss key findings

### Knowledge check 15

What levels of measurement are the following?
- Observer ratings of attractiveness
- Number of people answering yes in a referendum
- Number of errors in a proofreading task
- IQ scores
- Time taken to sort a pack of cards

### Knowledge check 16

Think of three ways to measure driving skill: one using nominal data, one using ordinal data and one using interval data.

### Evaluation: qualitative data

**Strengths**
- Focus on meaning and experience
- Allow people's own voices to be heard
- Rich and detailed

**Weaknesses**
- Can be complex to analyse and compare
- May rely more on interpretation by the researcher
- The research methods used (self report) may lead to demand characteristics

**Exam tip**

Make sure that you can explain both qualitative and quantitative data. Try to find examples of each in the research that you have studied.

# Primary and secondary data

Primary data are data that are collected by researchers through their investigations. These would include data collected from questionnaires, interviews, observations and experiments. Secondary data are data that already exist and the researcher simply uses these already existing data. These could include official statistics (e.g. in relation to health, education or crime), data collected from other sources (e.g. football scores) or data included in already existing sources such as letters and diaries.

**Exam tip**

See if you can identify any secondary data in any of the research you have studied. You could use this as an example if you had to describe secondary data in the examination.

# Descriptive statistics

Psychological research produces data, which need to be understood and interpreted. Descriptive statistics allow us to describe and summarise the data that we have collected while inferential statistics allow us to make inferences and draw conclusions from our results.

# Measures of central tendency

## Mean

The mean is calculated by adding all the scores together and then dividing by the number of scores. This is a useful statistic as it takes all the scores into account, but it can be misleading if there are one or more extreme scores all in the same direction.

For example, the mean of the following scores would not be very helpful:

8, 10, 10, 12, 60

The mean of 100, 101, 99, 102, 98, 100 is 100.

The mean of 100, 40, 120, 60, 180, 100 is also 100, but the mean in this case would not reflect the very different distribution of scores.

## Median

The median is the mid-point that separates the higher 50% of the scores from the lower 50% of the scores.

The median of 2, 4, 6, 8, 19 is 6.

This is often a more useful measure than the mean when there are extreme scores or a skewed distribution. It does not, however, work well with small data sets and can be affected by any alteration of the central values (but not the extreme ones).

For example, if we have two sets of data:

10, 12, 13, 14, 18, 19, 22, 22

10, 12, 13, 14, 15, 19, 22, 22

The median would be 16 in the first case and 14.5 in the second case, despite only one value being different in the two sets of data. Note that the median would stay the same if the final value was 222.

## Mode

The mode is the score that occurs most often. It is possible to have more than one mode — a set of data with two modes is called bimodal and a set of data with more than two modes is called multimodal. The mode can be useful where other figures may be meaningless. For example, it might make more sense to know the most common response to a question rather than the mean response. However, the mode does have its limitations and when there are only a few scores representing each value, very small changes can dramatically alter the mode.

For example:

3, 6, 8, 9, 10, 10 mode = 10

3, 3, 6, 8, 9, 10 mode = 3

However, the mode will always be a value that exists in the data which is not necessarily true of other measures of central tendency.

# Measures of variability or dispersion

The range is the difference between the smallest and the largest number in a set of scores. It is a fairly crude measure of variability since it only takes the highest and lowest scores into account and so one very high or very low score can distort the data.

The standard deviation (SD) is a statistical measure of dispersion. The standard deviation tells us how much, on average, scores differ from the mean score. A large SD tells us that the spread of scores is wide; a small SD tells us that the scores are clustered around the mean.

## Frequency distribution curves: normal distributions and skewed distributions

A frequency distribution curve gives us a visual representation of variability and tells us how frequently each score occurs. Some frequency distribution curves produce a symmetrical bell-shaped curve known as a normal distribution. A normal distribution has the following properties: the mean, median and mode all occur at the same point and the distribution of scores is identical each side of the mean. Not all sets of scores are normally distributed. Sometimes distributions are skewed, either negatively or positively. A positive skew occurs when most of the scores fall below the mean and a negative skew occurs when most of the scores fall above the mean.

**Exam tip**

The spread of scores may seem obvious in the kind of small-scale research that you might conduct, but large-scale research projects have such large data sets that it impossible to simply look at the results and see that the data are all very close together or very spread out. This ability to make estimations is a very useful one but becomes more and difficult when data sets get very large.

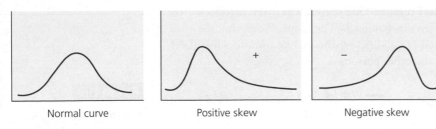

| Normal curve | Positive skew | Negative skew |

**Figure 3** Normal, positively skewed and negatively skewed distribution curves

A typical examination question might ask you to sketch a summary table of the following results:

Time (in seconds) to complete a jigsaw puzzle

| Quiet condition | Noisy condition |
|---|---|
| 20 | 26 |
| 22 | 26 |
| 22 | 28 |
| 24 | 28 |
| 24 | 30 |
| 26 | 30 |

Being asked to sketch a summary table means that the examiner does not want to see the raw data. Instead, you could calculate the mean, the median or the mode of these data and present them in a small table. It would also be appropriate to use the totals for each condition, but in the examples below the mean has been used. The means work out as 23 and 28. Now you need to think about the best way to present these figures. What is missing from the table below?

| | Condition A | Condition B |
|---|---|---|
| **Average** | 23 | 28 |

The problem with this table is that it has not been labelled correctly. It is impossible to draw a conclusion from it as you do not know what the unit of the average is: seconds, centimetres, the number of questions answered correctly, the number of mistakes made etc. Neither do you know what the conditions are. You would lose a lot of marks if you drew this in the examination. The table below has complete labels.

**Average time** (in seconds) taken to complete a puzzle

| Quiet room | Noisy room |
|---|---|
| 23 | 28 |

# Graphs

There are a range of different graphs which can be used to display your data. However, it is crucial to select the right one and to ensure that you label everything correctly.

## Line graphs

A line graph is a way of demonstrating change, usually over time, by a series of points joined up into a line. The graph below shows data collected in an experiment to see how accurately people could estimate 1 minute. One person was given feedback after each trial and one person was not given any feedback. The graph shows that the person given feedback slowly improved her ability to estimate one minute while there was little change in the estimates of the other person.

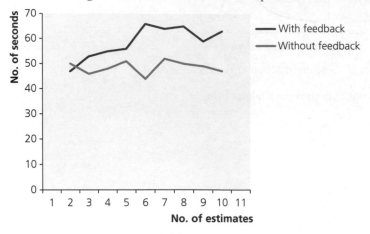

**Figure 4** Line graph to show estimates of 60 seconds with and without feedback

## Pie charts

A pie chart is a useful way to display percentages. For example, if you had conducted a simple survey to find out how your fellow students travelled to college you might display the results like this:

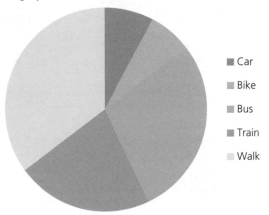

**Figure 5** Pie chart to show how students travel to college

## Bar charts and histograms

A bar chart displays data in categories and is probably the most familiar type of graph. We will look at some examples later in this section. It is important to understand the difference between a bar chart and a histogram. A bar chart displays data in categories and so a bar chart is drawn with a gap between the bars. A histogram, on the other hand, displays continuous data. For example, if you had recorded how long it took people to complete a task and had then divided this into 1–10 seconds, 11–20 seconds, 21–30 seconds and so on, these would be continuous data and a histogram (without the gaps between the bars) would be more appropriate.

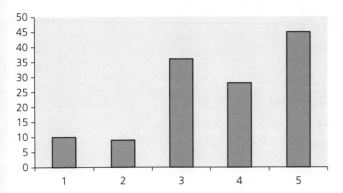

**Figure 6** A bar chart

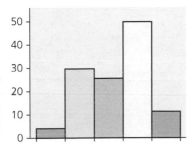

**Figure 7** A histogram

# Scatter graphs

You would only draw a scatter graph for a correlation and not for any other investigation. Scatter graphs display the relationship between two variables. However it is important to label these appropriately. The scatter graph below (see Figure 8) tells us nothing as we do not know what any of the variables are. You would get a maximum of 1 mark for drawing this.

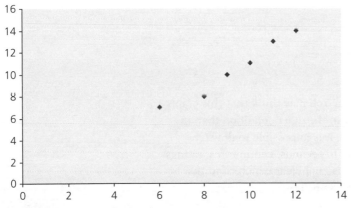

**Figure 8**

The next scatter graph in Figure 9 is much clearer. Now it is possible to draw the conclusion that there is a positive correlation between the estimated score and the actual score on a memory task.

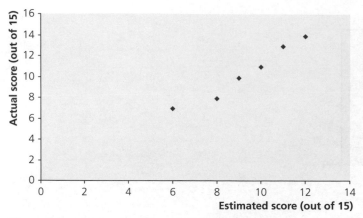

**Figure 9** A graph to show the relationship between estimated score and actual score on a memory test

## Drawing graphs in the examination

In the examination, you might also be asked to *sketch* a graph. The word 'sketch' is used to let you know that you do not have to draw this precisely. There are marks for selecting the appropriate graph and for labelling this correctly, but none for presentation. Again, the means have been used here, but you could use totals instead. What is missing from the bar chart below (see Figure 10)?

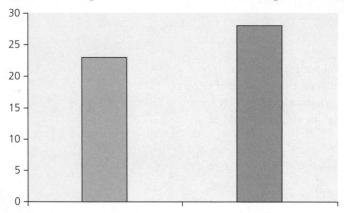

**Figure 10**

What conclusions can you draw from the graph above? You may think that this graph displays clearly that people completed the task faster in the quiet condition than in the noisy condition, but since it has not been labelled, it is impossible to draw any conclusions from the graph. The numbers could refer to seconds, centimetres, ratings of something or number of words remembered. It is also not clear which condition is which. The graph below has been fully labelled (see Figure 11).

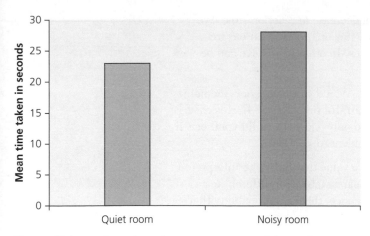

**Figure 11** A graph to show the mean amount of time taken to complete a puzzle in a quiet room compared to a noisy room

Here we have a properly labelled graph. Now we can draw a conclusion that on average, participants completed a puzzle faster in a quiet room than in a noisy room. This bar chart would be awarded full marks in an examination.

# Inferential statistics

When we carry out a psychological investigation we usually have TWO hypotheses: the **null hypothesis** which states that the results will be due to chance, and the **experimental (alternate) hypothesis** which predicts that the results are due to the manipulation of the variable being studied.

Which one of these hypotheses offers the best explanation for our results? We cannot prove one to be correct but we can make an intelligent guess about the most likely explanation. This is called an **inference**. We want to assess the probability that our results could be due to chance factors. To do this, we need to use inferential statistics.

For example, if we carry out a study on the effects of alcohol on reaction time, we might obtain the following results:
- Average time to sort a pack of playing cards into suits:
  - with alcohol 38 seconds
  - without alcohol 34 seconds

We need to know whether this 4 seconds difference in performance is due to the effects of the alcohol, or whether it is due to the variation caused by chance effects. Statistics tell us the probability that the null hypothesis could explain our results, in other words, the probability or likelihood that the results are due to chance.

# Probability and significance levels

It is an academic convention in psychology that we accept the null hypothesis as the best explanation of the results unless there is only a 5% (or less) probability of the results being due to chance. This is written as $p < 0.05$. If our statistical test tells us that the probability of the results being due to chance is less than 5% then we can reject the null hypothesis and accept the experimental (alternate) hypothesis.

However, we have not proved that alcohol caused a decrease in reaction time. We have inferred a causal link and there is a probability (5% or 1 in 20) that we are wrong and that the results simply occurred by chance. In other words, we can be 95% confident in this conclusion.

Sometimes we need to be more than 95% confident. Would you take a new medicine if the doctor said she was 95% sure that it had no harmful side effects? In this case, we might use a more stringent significance level and only reject the null hypothesis if we are 99% confident ($p < 0.01$) or even 99.9% confident ($p < 0.001$).

Whatever statistical test you use, you will calculate a value that has to be interpreted using a significance table. There are specific significance tables for different tests. Interpreting the value will give you a level of significance, that is, a probability that the results occurred by chance.

If $p < 0.05$ this means that there is a 1 in 20 probability that the results occurred by chance. If $p < 0.01$ this means that there is a 1 in 100 probability that the results occurred by chance. This gives you a higher level of confidence in rejecting the null hypothesis.

# Type 1 and Type 2 errors

Because we can never be 100% sure that our results are due to chance, it is possible that we might reject our null hypothesis and accept our experimental hypothesis when the results were in fact a chance occurrence. This is termed a Type 1 error. If we were to accept the null hypothesis and reject the experimental hypothesis when in fact the results were due to our experimental manipulation, this would be termed a Type 2 error.

The more stringent the level of significance chosen, the more likely we are to make a Type 2 error. The 0.01 level of significance states that we can only accept the experimental (alternate) hypothesis if there is a 1 in 100 probability (or less) that the results are due to chance. If we make the level of significance a stringent one in order to avoid making a Type 1 error then we automatically increase the risk of making a Type 2 error. On the other hand, if we use a more lenient level of probability (say 0.1 or 1 in 10) then we reduce the likelihood of making a Type 2 error but increase the probability of making a Type 1 error.

The 0.05 level is commonly used in psychology as it is thought to offer the best balance between making a Type 1 and Type 2 error.

# Choosing a statistical test

In order to decide which test is the correct one to use, you need to know the level of measurement (see page 26) and the design of the study. Once you have this information you can use the table below to select the correct test.

Having interval or ratio level data may allow you to use more sensitive tests than those designed for nominal or ordinal data. These are called parametric tests, but the following conditions need to be met:

■ The data need to be interval or ratio.
■ The data should be normally distributed (see pages 28 and 29).

■ There should be homogeneity of variance. This means that the variability of the two sets of scores should be similar. This can be calculated by working out the variance ($SD^2$) for both sets of data.

If you have interval or ratio level data but you have not met the other requirements for a parametric test, you will analyse your data using the test for ordinal data and the appropriate design. These tests are called non-parametric tests. This means that the first step in your analysis will be to rank order your data.

**NB** Some types of data (such as attitude scales and IQ tests) may look like interval data but are best treated as ordinal as the intervals between the units on the scale are not necessarily equal.

| Design | Level of data | | |
|---|---|---|---|
| | Nominal | Ordinal | Interval |
| Test of difference with repeated measures (and matched pairs) | Sign test | Wilcoxon sign test | Related t-test |
| Test of difference with independent measures | Chi-squared | Mann–Whitney U-test | Unrelated t-test |
| Correlation | Chi-squared | Spearman's rho | Pearson product moment |

**Knowledge check 17**

Identify the most appropriate test for each of the following:
- repeated measures and ordinal level data
- correlation and interval level (parametric) data
- repeated measures and interval level (parametric) data
- independent measures and nominal data
- independent measures and interval level (parametric) data
- correlation and ordinal level data
- independent measures and ordinal level data

# Methodological issues

## Representativeness and generalisability

These issues have already been covered in the sections on sampling and sampling techniques (see pages 15, 16 and 17). It is obviously very important that in any piece of research we are able to generalise our findings beyond the specific sample that we have tested. This requires our sample to be as representative of the target population as possible. For example, if we selected all our participants from an art class in a sixth form college, we would be unwise to generalise those findings to all the students of the college, because the art students may not be representative of the college population as a whole.

**Knowledge check 18**

Identify a Core Study where it may be difficult to generalise from the sample that was selected. Explain why this is the case.

# Reliability

Reliability means consistency. In experimental research, this refers to the ability to replicate a piece of research. Assuming that a study is replicated exactly, we would expect to achieve very similar results. This is why it is so important that researchers publish details of their procedures — so other psychologists can see exactly what they have done and may attempt to replicate their findings.

Reliability can also mean consistency of measurements. In the examination, you are most likely to meet this issue when considering observational research.

## Inter-rater reliability

If an observation has high inter-rater reliability, this means that two or more observers are agreed on how behaviour should be categorised. In other words, it does not matter who conducts the observation since all the observers would record the same information.

You can improve the inter-rater reliability by making the categories as clear and unambiguous as possible and by training those observing to use the coding scheme that you have designed specifically for the observation. You can also conduct pilot studies to test out the coding scheme to see if it accounts for all the behaviour that you are likely to see and to identify any problems that might arise.

The reliability of tests can be measured in the following ways:

- **Split-half reliability.** Here, scores on half the test items are correlated with scores on the other half of the test items. Since items on some tests may get progressively more difficult, it is common practice to correlate scores on even numbered items with scores on odd numbered items. High split-half reliability means that a test is internally consistent.
- **Test-retest reliability.** The same group is tested on two separate occasions and the two scores are correlated. This can be problematic if the two test occasions are close together as people may remember how they answered the first time. This would also apply to measures of abilities such as perception or memory. It is difficult to re-test people on the same material as it produces a number of biases (see later in this section).

> **Exam tip**
>
> Make sure that you can define reliability without using the word 'reliable'.

# Validity

Validity means accuracy. A measure is valid if it is testing what we want it to test. It is possible to evaluate the validity of a measurement as well as that of a procedure in general. You may well be asked to suggest improvements or alternatives to forms of measurement in the exam and then to consider their effects. Think in terms of accuracy: will your improvement lead to a more accurate result? Why? For example, in a questionnaire, were the questions worded clearly enough, or might people have interpreted them as meaning something else? This would lower the validity.

You will not be asked about ways of measuring validity, but these include **split-half** (for example, comparing the results from one half of the questionnaire with those from the other half) and **test-retest** (giving the same test to the same people on two occasions and correlating the results).

You might wish to consider the validity of the research in more general terms. This can be subdivided as follows:

- **Internal validity.** In terms of an experiment, did the independent variable really have an effect on the dependent variable, or were there some significant confounding variables that have not been controlled for? In a questionnaire, this might include looking at more general aspects of the procedure: could people see each other's questionnaires or hear each other's responses? Would they respond to demand characteristics or be influenced by social desirability bias?
- **External validity.** Can the results be generalised beyond the specific study that has been conducted? This could be considered in terms of **population validity** (the extent to which it would be appropriate to generalise the findings to a wider group of people) or **ecological validity** (the extent to which the findings of this specific study can be generalised to other settings or situations).

There are a number of ways in which the validity of a measure (or a test) can be established. These include:

- **Face/content validity.** This simply refers to whether the test seems, on the face of it, to be measuring what it claims to be measuring. For example, if an intelligence test contained only mathematics questions, we might question whether it was really testing intelligence.
- **Concurrent validity.** This involves correlating the test scores with another independent measure of the same variable. So scores from a new personality test may be correlated with scores from an existing test.
- **Predictive validity.** This involves correlating the results of a test with some measure of future performance. This is very common for example in education as well as in many occupations. Exam results could be used to predict how well someone might do on a higher level course or in a particular job. If the exams turn out not to predict future performance then they lack validity and usefulness.
- **Construct validity.** This refers to the extent to which our commonsense notions and psychological knowledge indicate that a test is measuring what it purports to be measuring. For example, a test of anxiety should show high scores when people are tested prior to an examination (or jumping out of an aeroplane!) and low scores when people are relaxing at home.

# Bias and demand characteristics

People do not agree to take part in psychological research and then think no more about it. They try to work out what is going on and what the experimenter might be expecting of them. This can produce several effects: the participants either attempt to please the experimenter and produce the behaviour that they think he or she wants, or they do the exact opposite of what they think he or she expects them to do. This has been referred to as the **'screw you effect'**. There is a third possibility: the participants are concerned that the experimenter is judging them and so they try hard to appear 'normal'.

> **Exam tip**
>
> These issues are important to keep in mind when you are evaluating or designing research. Ask yourself what factors might be influencing the participants in such a way that their behaviour is not that which you would observe if they were unaware of being tested.

> **Exam tip**
>
> This might all seem very complex but these are just a range of ways in which we can try to determine whether a psychological measure is measuring what it claims to.

> **Knowledge check 19**
>
> Think about the personality quizzes that you see on Facebook or in magazines. To what extent do you think these are valid?

> **Knowledge check 20**
>
> Think about the Core Study by Bandura et al. Did this study have ecological validity? If you are studying A-level, you could answer the same question about the study by Piliavin et al.

# Social desirability

Social desirability is a similar issue to demand characteristics and is probably most relevant to self-report methods. For example, if you were asking questions about parents' use of punishment, you would be unlikely to get the truth from everybody as people would be concerned with the way that they are presenting themselves. This might lead them to say that they do not punish their children when in fact they do. Would you tell the truth if your tutor conducted a survey to find out how much time people spent on their homework?

**Knowledge check 21**

Identify potential social desirability effects in any research that you have studied.

# Researcher/observer bias

Bias can occur in many different ways in psychological research, for example in the way that a question is worded or that an observer categorises behaviour. It is possible that the person conducting the research has an idea of what he or she is hoping to find, and even in the most tightly controlled experimental research, bias might be present, for example in the way that the experimenter communicates with participants. Moreover, giving participants full details of the research before they start, while ethical, can often influence the way that they behave.

Bias can be reduced by piloting questionnaires to ensure that the meaning is clear, training observers in the use of coding schemes, using multiple observers and ensuring that there is a high level of inter-rater reliability, and even by using single-blind or double-blind procedures.

**Knowledge check 22**

Identify one piece of research where the observer or researcher may have had significant effects on the behaviour of the participants. Would it be possible to reduce these effects?

> **Exam tip**
>
> A single-blind procedure is one where the participants are unaware of the aims of the research (however, while this may reduce bias, it may also produce ethical problems). A double-blind procedure is one where a second experimenter is used to gather the data — one who has no knowledge of the aims of the research. This significantly reduces the possibility of the experimenter being able to bias the research.

> **Exam tip**
>
> You can read the most recent Code of Ethics and Conduct by visiting the British Psychological Society's website at www.bps.org.uk and typing 'code of conduct' into the search box.

# Ethical considerations

All psychological research needs to conform to the Code of Ethics and Conduct produced by the British Psychological Society.

The code is based on four ethical principles:
- respect
- competence
- responsibility
- integrity

> **Exam tip**
>
> Look these words up if you are not sure what they mean.

The key guidelines for students conducting research or considering the research conducted by others are as follows:

- Participants should give informed consent prior to taking part in psychological research.
- Participants have the right to withdraw from research at any time.
- Participants should be fully debriefed.
- All information held on participants should be confidential.
- Participants should not be placed at risk of short- or long-term harm.

If you are conducting research as part of your preparation for this examination, you should not:
- ask people about aspects of their personal lives, such as involvement in illegal activities, sexuality or other private issues
- use children under 16 as your participants
- conduct any investigation where you are putting people into conditions that might cause them distress or embarrassment

However, if you were evaluating a piece of research in terms of ethics, you should consider the following:

- Is there any likelihood of the participants being distressed or embarrassed by the research?
- Are the participants at any risk of short- or long-term harm?
- Have they given their informed consent?
- Are they able to withdraw from the research?

You could also consider the implications of some of the guidelines on the research being conducted. For example, if people know that they are being observed, this might affect the way they behave. However, if we do not tell them that we are observing them, we might be breaking the ethical guidelines.

**Knowledge check 23**

Which studies that you have covered do you think are the most unethical? Make sure that you can explain why.

**Knowledge check 24**

Which studies are the most ethical? Explain why you have chosen these.

**Exam tip**

It is acceptable to observe people 'in a public place', but 'public place' has never been fully defined. Would you be happy to be observed without your knowledge by a psychologist or a psychology student?

## Summary

- There are many ways of presenting data but it is important to make sure that the type of graph or descriptive statistic that you use is appropriate for the data that you have.
- Statistical tests give you the probability that the results could have occurred by chance. Different tests are appropriate for different types of data and for different experimental designs.

- There are a range of evaluation issues which can be applied to the research you have studied as well as the research that you have conducted. Make sure you can see which ones are most appropriate for each piece of research and be prepared to apply these issues to different scenarios in the examination.

# ■ Report writing

## Sections and subsections of a practical report

There is no point in doing psychological research unless the findings are shared with other psychologists. When research is published it is validated by other psychologists (this is the process of peer review, considered later) and becomes part of the permanent scientific record. Published reports in psychology are composed of a series of sections. Each section includes specific details which allow for the information to be conveyed precisely and clearly to the readers.

**Report sections**

| Section | Function |
| --- | --- |
| Title | To tell the reader what the report is about |
| Abstract | To provide the reader with a brief summary of the study |
| Introduction | To introduce the background and rationale of the study |
| Method | To describe the way that the study will be conducted |
| Results | To present and summarise the findings including any statistical analysis |
| Discussion | To discuss the findings and their implications |
| References/bibliography | To inform the reader about the sources of information used |
| Appendices | Can be used for detailed information not in the report |

## The title

The report title is important because it will determine who reads the full report. It should be as concise as possible yet at the same time it should be informative. Anyone reading the title should know exactly what the report is about. This means that in most cases titles of academic reports are quite long rather than being short and snappy like a newspaper headline.

## Abstract

An abstract of a scientific report should be a brief (150 words) summary of the report. If a psychologist finds the title to be useful the next step is for him or her to read the abstract which is a concise summary of the study covering the aims/hypothesis, method/procedure, results and conclusions. Although you can generally find the abstracts of all published research online, you may not be able to access any more than this without a subscription to the journal or a one-off payment. This makes the abstract even more important when trying to decide whether you need to access the full article.

## Introduction

The introduction is designed to introduce the reader to the topic area and background to the study. This is made up largely of the relevant theories and past studies/research relevant to the research question. This allows the reader to place the study in context and allows the researcher to introduce the actual study and to explain the ideas behind

**Exam tip**

Read the titles of some of the studies that you have covered and consider whether they adequately explain what the studies are about.

**Exam tip**

Try to write abstracts for some of the research that you are familiar with. If you have access to the full text of a study you could read the abstract after you have written your own to see how similar they are.

it before going into the specific research predictions (hypotheses). You do not include any information about the method that is going to be used here.

## Method

This section describes how the study was conducted. It should have enough information to allow for **replication**. This serves two important functions: if the method cannot be replicated then the findings cannot be checked to see if they are (1) **reliable** and (2) **valid**.

This section comprises a number of subsections including the design, participants, apparatus/resources/materials, pilot study and procedure. It is important to include as much relevant information as possible.

## Results

This section reports the findings of the study clearly and accurately. It is typically made up of two sections: **descriptive** (allows for visual representation of differences between the groups) and **inferential** (analysis of the data and decisions on whether the null hypothesis is to be accepted or rejected). See 29 and 33 for information on descriptive and inferential statistics.

## Discussion

This section begins with a summary of the findings of the results before going on to an exploration of the best explanations of the findings. The researcher offers explanations of the findings, considers possible weaknesses and improvements as well as the implications of the research and suggestions for further research. This may be followed by a conclusion in some reports.

## References/bibliography

This is where the authors give details of all research documents, journals, internet resources and books that were cited in the report. A brief outline of referencing using the Harvard referencing system (although APA referencing is standard in most psychology journals) is given later in this section.

## Appendices

This section comprises the resources/materials used within the study, raw data and statistical calculations. It is rare to see this in journal articles, but it is standard practice for students to include this material in assessed reports.

## Citing academic references

Referencing is a way for authors to acknowledge the published work that they have referred to in their work. There is more to this than simply adding a list of books and articles to the end of an assignment. Referencing involves a citation within your work to show the source of information usually a name and date in brackets after the information for example (Jones, 2010). This name and date should also appear in your reference list where you would give the full reference for the source (this could be a book, an article, a website or one of a range of other sources).

**Exam tip**

Look in the back of a textbook or at the end of a journal article to see an example of a reference section.

# References

Your list of references appears alphabetically by author at the end of your document. The exact format depends on whether you are referencing a book, an article or some other source. The punctuation and the emphasis given to sections of the typeface is of great importance.

An example of a book reference:

Lintern, F. (2015) *OCR Psychology Student Guide 1*, Philip Allan for Hodder Education

An example of a journal reference:

Della Sala, S. (2015) 'Science and pseudoscience', *Psychology Review*, 20 (3), 25–27

# Peer review

Research is published in academic journals such as the *British Journal of Psychology*. These journals are referred to as 'peer reviewed' as they have a rigorous process of reviewing and checking submitted papers before they are published. This process consists of papers being anonymised before being sent to other respected academics working in similar areas for their comments. They are asked to comment on the quality not only of the written report but also of the research that has been conducted. They may simply agree that the research is of a sufficient quality to be published as it is, or they may have questions or suggestions for changes. They may of course, also respond by saying that that the research is not of a sufficient quality to be published in the journal.

This process has several advantages. It is a type of 'quality control' which ensures that only well-conducted and well-written research makes it into the journals. This in turn means that you, as a reader, can be reassured that you are reading high quality research. With the number of open access journals now available online, meaning that anyone can publish without this review process, this is an important strength of peer review.

However, the system is not without its flaws. Some critics argue that this process does not prevent poor quality, flawed research from being published. Some research areas are very small and it may be difficult to find appropriate (objective) reviewers to review the research. It may also be obvious to the reviewer who has written the article he or she is reviewing and if they are rivals in a research area, the reviewer may be more critical.

---

**Knowledge check 25**

Look up plagiarism. Why do you think that plagiarism is such an important issue in academia?

**Exam tip**

You can use the referencing tool in Word to create your own reference list.

**Exam tip**

If you are planning to go on to university you will need to develop excellent referencing skills. Referencing not only shows that you have conducted good research and that you have used the material that you have researched to develop your own arguments, it also shows that you can back up the information and arguments that you have presented. A well referenced piece of work will have a strong academic style and this will be reflected in the marks that you receive.

---

## Summary

- In this section we have examined the way that a piece of research should be reported as well as the appropriate way to reference the material that you have used. We have also looked at the process of peer review.

- Make sure that you can describe report writing, referencing and peer review as all these topics could come up in the examination.

# ■ Practical activities

Although this component will not directly examine the research that you have conducted yourself, you are advised to conduct as many practical activities as possible as it is much easier to understand the principles of good research design if you have tried it yourself. So, if possible, try to collect data using the four techniques required for the examination. The ideas outlined below will help you.

## Experiment

Experiments have already been discussed in this book. For now, simply remember that to conduct an experiment you need to collect data in two conditions. This means that you have an **independent variable**, which differs between the two conditions, and a **dependent variable**, which is measured in both conditions. The independent variable could be experimentally manipulated (such as noisy and quiet conditions) or could be naturally occurring (such as maths students compared to art students on a particular task). You should keep the conditions relatively simple. Avoid the temptation to have more than two conditions, as this can get extremely complicated.

If you have different people in each condition of your investigation, this is described as an **independent measures design**.

### Suggestions for independent measures design experiments

- Do people have better memory (or attention or reaction time) in quiet or noisy conditions?
- How does the use of different words in questions affect memory (e.g. you could see how verbs such as 'hit' or 'smashed' affect estimates of reaction time, or how words such as 'group' or 'crowd' affect estimates of the number of people)?
- Are words paired with visual images of these words remembered better than words alone?
- How do small changes in information (name, age, description) affect the impression formed of that person?

If you test the same people twice (i.e. once under each condition), this is called a **repeated measures design**.

### Suggestions for repeated measures design tests

- A reaction-time test, with and without an audience
- A memory test, comparing people's memory in the morning and the afternoon
- An eyewitness-testimony test, comparing people's memory straight after witnessing an event and a day or a week later
- Test to see how many press-ups someone completes alone and then in competition with someone else

Note that some of the above suggestions could be conducted as either independent measures or repeated measures designs. You would need to think about the advantages and disadvantages of using each design (this is discussed in more detail on page 18).

# Self-report

This can be any data-collecting activity that involves questioning people directly. It could be a survey of attitudes to something, or a questionnaire asking people about themselves or some aspect of their behaviour. Plan your questions carefully and try them out on a small group of people before you ask your participants to make sure that everyone understands the questions in the same way. This is called a 'pilot study'. Make sure that you avoid any questions that might embarrass or offend people.

### Ideas for questionnaires

- Ask students about their study habits.
- Ask students about their sleep habits.
- Ask students (or teachers) about daily hassles (minor stress).
- Measure attitudes to TV violence.
- Measure attitudes to crime and punishment.
- Find out how helpful people might be in different circumstances.

# Observation

This activity involves the design of a coding scheme (or set of categories) to record a particular behaviour. The behaviour can be anything at all, but do not forget that there are ethical guidelines restricting where it is acceptable to observe people without their consent. Try to keep your coding scheme relatively simple — it is not necessary to have more than four or five categories, and you may have even fewer than that.

### Suggestions for observations

- Animal behaviour (many zoos/wildlife parks have information on primate behaviour, which might allow you to develop a coding scheme to observe such behaviour as mother–infant interaction, time use, grooming and facial expressions)
- Superstitious behaviour — do more people walk around a ladder or under it?
- What people do with their litter
- How male and female students spend their 'free time' in college/school
- How people display aggressive behaviour on the sports field
- The use of mobile phones by gender and age

# Correlation

Correlation is more a method of data analysis than it is a research method. To conduct a correlation, you simply need to measure two variables that you think might be related in some way.

If you think that two variables will increase in line with each other (such as how much football someone watched on TV and their score in a football general knowledge quiz), this is predicting a **positive correlation**. If you think that the variables will move in opposite directions (such as how many hours of sleep someone has had and how long it takes him or her to complete a task), you are predicting a **negative correlation**.

You can use a variety of techniques to measure the variables, such as self-reports and observations, as well as tests of ability. Note that all you are predicting is a *relationship* — not that a change in one variable *causes* a change in the other. In a correlation, you are not manipulating anything and cannot draw conclusions about cause and effect. You would need to conduct an experiment (where one variable is manipulated and its effect on another variable is measured) to reach this kind of conclusion.

## Suggestions for correlation activities

- Is there a relationship between the number of hours of sleep someone has had and his or her performance on a reaction-time task?
- Is there a relationship between regular viewing of soap operas and score on a memory task based on watching one episode?
- Is there a relationship between a personality measure (such as extroversion) and another variable (such as how many times an individual goes out each week, or how long he or she spends on the phone each week)?
- Is there a relationship between a person's estimate of how good his or her memory is and the score that he or she achieves on a memory test?

## Summary

- The more research you conduct the more you will grasp the principles of research design. Try to conduct at least one piece of research using each of the four techniques covered here.
- Think about the problems you encountered in designing or conducting your research. This will help you to understand the strengths and weaknesses of the different techniques.

# ■ How science works

What does it mean to say that psychology is a science? In broad terms this means that psychologists use the **scientific method** when investigating their research questions:

- The scientific method involves the collection of data through carefully constructed experiments and observations (rather than relying on attitudes or beliefs).
- It relies on hypothesis testing and the manipulation and control of variables.
- Researchers using the scientific method should be objective and unbiased in their approaches.

If all these aspects of the scientific method are followed, we should be confident in our ability to draw **cause and effect relationships**. This means that we can be sure that one variable (the IV) is having an effect on another variable (the DV). Remember that you can only draw this conclusion if you have investigated this experimentally (by **manipulating** the IV and measuring its effect on the DV) using the scientific method. Using a non-experimental method or failing to control confounding variables would mean that this cause and effect relationship cannot be drawn. The more **control** that the experimenter has over the IV and over the potential confounding variables the safer the conclusions are.

**Objectivity** refers to researchers trying to ensure that none of their personal values, opinions, beliefs or expectations has any influence on what they are doing. The opposite of objectivity is subjectivity — where researchers allow these factors to colour their perceptions.

**Replicability** means that research can be repeated (replicated). The more objective a piece of research is and the more control there is over potential confounding variables (as well as how accurately the research has been reported), the more likely is it that something can be replicated. Laboratory studies are obviously easier to replicate than naturalistic observations or case studies.

The scientific method is sometimes called the hypothetico-deductive method as shown in Figure 12.

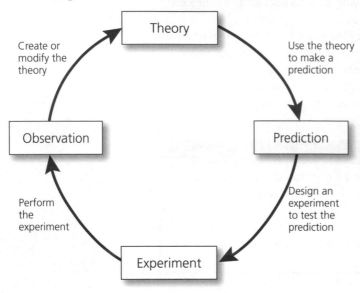

**Figure 12** The hypothetico-deductive method

Reasoning can be **deductive** or **inductive**. **Inductive reasoning** is the process of drawing generalised statements from a number of observations. This is how ideas about human behaviour become statements that can be tested. For example, a teacher might notice that her students complete less work when the temperature in the classroom falls below a certain point. After observing this on several occasions, she may draw the general conclusion that students work better in warm rooms than in cold rooms. She has not proved this — she has simply collected a number of observations that confirm her original ideas.

The scientific method would go further than this. Inductive reasoning would produce the idea (students work better in warm rooms) which could become a testable hypothesis. If this was then tested experimentally (with high levels of control and low levels of bias), **deductive reasoning** might allow us to conclude that the temperature of the room was a significant factor in explaining the amount of work that students do.

The notion of **falsification** goes even further than this. Although in practice science tends to work by researchers looking to confirm their hypothesis, Karl Popper suggested that good science should aim to falsify hypotheses rather than confirm

**Exam tip**

Make sure that you understand the difference between induction and deduction.

them. This is because however many times you see something happening you cannot prove that it will always happen like this. However, one occurrence of something not happening in the way that you predicted does disprove a hypothesis and this means that the hypothesis needs to be amended. This is how science (and psychology) makes progress.

## Summary

- The scientific method consists of collecting data in controlled, objective experiments which test hypotheses.
- Manipulation of variables in experiments reveals cause and effect relationships.
- Research should be replicable.

# Questions & Answers

## Skills required for the examination

Three skills — the **assessment objectives** (AOs) — are assessed in the examinations and are as follows:

| AO1 | Demonstrate knowledge and understanding of scientific ideas, processes, techniques and procedures |
|---|---|
| AO2 | Apply knowledge and understanding of scientific ideas, processes, techniques and procedures: <br> ■ in a theoretical context <br> ■ in a practical context <br> ■ when handling qualitative data <br> ■ when handling quantitative data |
| AO3 | Analyse, interpret and evaluate scientific information, ideas and evidence, including in relation to issues, to: <br> ■ make judgements and reach conclusions <br> ■ develop and refine practical design and procedures |

## Examination guidance

The AS examination is 1 hour and 30 minutes long and is worth 75 marks, and the A-level examination is 2 hours long and is worth 90 marks. Whichever one you are sitting, the examination paper will comprise *three* sections — sections A, B and C. You are required to answer *all* the questions in each section.

### Section A: multiple choice

Questions from across the Component 1 content. Questions could also relate to the research methods used in the core studies.

(AS: 15 questions and 15 marks; A-level: 20 questions and 20 marks)

### Section B: research design and response

Assessment will focus on a novel source. The themes for questions will be:
■ the planning and design of research
■ the evaluation of research
■ improvements to research

(AS: 7 short questions and 1 longer question, 35 marks; A-level: 4 short questions and 1 longer question, 35 marks)

### Section C: data analysis and interpretation

This section will require students to analyse and interpret novel data or a piece of hypothetical research using descriptive and/or inferential statistics.

(AS: 7 short questions, 25 marks; A-level: 7 short questions, 35 marks)

## Advice for the examination

Some questions require short answers, a definition for 2 marks for example, while others, such as a 'describe' and 'evaluate' question part, will require more detail. You therefore need to think about how much you need to write in each answer to guarantee all the marks. One sentence will clearly not be enough for a 12- or 15-mark question, but conversely do not waste time writing a whole paragraph for a 'definition' question when a few words suffice.

Whatever you do, do not run out of time. Be strict with yourself. Try testing yourself at home so that you know exactly how much you can write in the time allowed. If you finish ahead of time, reread all your answers and see if you really have written as much and as clearly as you should have done.

Note that the OCR exams are marked online. This means that at the start of the exam you will be given an OCR question and answer booklet. You must write only within the lines on each page to make sure that the pages will scan correctly, otherwise the examiner may not receive your whole answer.

## Practice questions

This section is structured as follows:

- sample questions in the style of the component
- analysis of each question, explaining what is expected in each part of the question
- example student responses — these have been selected to illustrate particular strengths and limitations

Although both AS-type questions and A-level-type questions are included in this section, the specification content is the same for both, so whether you are studying for AS or A-level it would be useful revision to try all of the questions in this section.

## Exam comments

All student responses are followed by exam comments. These are preceded by the icon **ⓔ** and indicate where credit is due. In the weaker answers, they also point out areas for improvement, specific problems and common errors such as poor time management, lack of clarity, weak or non-existent development, irrelevance, misinterpretation of the question and mistaken meanings of terms. The comments also indicate how each example answer would be marked in an actual exam.

Commentary on the questions are preceded by the icon **ⓔ**. They offer tips on what you need to do to gain full marks.

# ■ Section A

## Multiple choice

### AS questions

15 questions and 15 marks

1  Which of the following is a definition of a null hypothesis?

   **A**  The aim of the study

   **B**  The statement of 'no effect'

   **C**  The prediction of what the researcher expects to find

   **D**  The opposite of what the researcher expects to find

2  Which type of graph would be used to display the results from a correlation?

   **A**  Bar chart           **C**  Scattergraph

   **B**  Line graph          **D**  Pie chart

3  If your questionnaire was accused of social desirability bias, what would this mean?

   **A**  People will be rude when they answer it

   **B**  People will throw it in the bin

   **C**  People will give the answers that they think they should give

   **D**  People will let someone else answer it for them

4  Look at the following table and then answer the question below.

| | Supports local football team | Does not support local football team |
|---|---|---|
| Male | 35 | 15 |
| Female | 5 | 45 |

   Which statistical test would be used to analyse these data?

   **A**  Chi-squared test      **C**  Sign test

   **B**  Mann–Whitney test    **D**  T-test

5  Where would you find details of the participants in a practical report?

   **A**  The introduction      **C**  The results

   **B**  The method         **D**  The discussion

6  Which of these is not an ethical issue?

   **A**  Confidentiality       **C**  Protection of participants

   **B**  Demand characteristics   **D**  Right to withdraw

7  If a researcher obtained her sample of participants from all those who were in the sixth form common room first thing in the morning, what would this sample be called?

   **A**  An opportunity sample    **C**  A snowball sample

   **B**  A random sample       **D**  A stratified sample

8 Which of these is a weakness of an opportunity sample?

   **A**  The sample will be too small

   **B**  The sample will be too big

   **C**  The sample will be representative of the target population

   **D**  The sample is unlikely to be representative of the target population

9 Before a research report is published in an academic journal, which of these processes take place?

   **A**  Peer assessment      **C**  An interview with the author

   **B**  Peer review           **D**  A payment to the author

10 A researcher includes the following question in an interview: 'Tell me what you think about the library in your school'. Is this:

   **A**  A closed question      **C**  A multiple-choice question

   **B**  Rating scale            **D**  An open question

11 Which of the following is an example of qualitative data?

   **A**  The number of people completing a task within a time limit

   **B**  The opinions people expressed about the task they had to do

   **C**  The number of mistakes people made in a task

   **D**  The number of people who failed to complete the task

12 Which design would be appropriate for a study comparing male and female abilities on a computer game?

   **A**  Repeated measures      **C**  Independent measures

   **B**  Case study            **D**  Correlation

13 Which of the following is a strength of quantitative data?

   **A**  They are rich and detailed

   **B**  They capture people's opinions in their own words

   **C**  They can easily be analysed statistically

   **D**  They cannot be analysed statistically

14 What is meant by 'observer bias'?

   **A**  The observer is allowing his or her own attitudes or expectations to influence their data recording

   **B**  The observer is not controlling what is going on

   **C**  The participants are not behaving in the way that the observer wants to

   **D**  There are not enough people to observe

15 Which of the following is not part of the scientific method?

   **A**  Hypothesis testing      **C**  Experimentation

   **B**  Objectivity            **D**  Subjectivity

# A-level questions

20 questions and 20 marks

**1** Which is the independent variable in the following hypothesis? 'People will complete more press-ups in 2 minutes when in competition than when working alone.'

**A** The number of press-ups someone can do

**B** 2 minutes

**C** Whether someone is completing the press-ups in competition or alone

**D** The number of people taking part

**2** A researcher collected data on how many people passed their driving test on their first attempt and how many people did not. What sort of data are these?

**A** Nominal                 **C** Internal

**B** Ordinal                   **D** Qualitative

**3** Which statistical test would be used to analyse data which were interval (parametric) and repeated measures?

**A** Mann–Whitney U-test       **C** Related t-test

**B** Unrelated t-test             **D** Chi-squared test

**4** What is meant by saying that an observational study showed high levels of inter-rater reliability?

**A** There is more than one observer

**B** There is only one observer

**C** There is a high positive correlation between the data collected by each observer

**D** There is a high negative correlation between the data collected by each observer

**5** A researcher wishes to interview parents whose children have recently left home about their feelings. The researcher identifies his first participant and then asks this person to suggest another person that he could approach. What term describes this type of sample?

**A** An opportunity sample     **C** A stratified sample

**B** A snowball sample          **D** A random sample

**6** A researcher times people completing episode one of Candy Crush (an online matching game). She collects the following data and decides to calculate the mean. What is the problem with selecting the mean for this?

| Participant | Time taken (secs) |
|:-----------:|:-----------------:|
| 1 | 45 |
| 2 | 56 |
| 3 | 39 |
| 4 | 66 |
| 5 | 58 |
| 6 | 178 |

**A** It will be hard to calculate

**B** You cannot calculate a mean of this type of data

**C** It will be skewed by the results from participant 6

**D** There are not enough participants

7   What does p<0.05 mean?

   **A**   That the probability of the results being due to chance is less than 1 in 20

   **B**   That the probability of the results being due to chance is more than 1 in 20

   **C**   That the probability of the results being due to chance is exactly 1 in 20

   **D**   That the probability of the results being due to chance is less than 1 in 200

8   What is meant by the statement that a researcher is risking making a Type 1 error?

   **A**   That their chosen significance level means that they might reject the null when they should have accepted it

   **B**   That their chosen significance level means that they might accept the null when they should have rejected it

   **C**   That they have used the wrong test

   **D**   That they have made mistakes in their calculations

9   Which of the following is a weakness of the process of peer review?

   **A**   It is expensive

   **B**   It is too complicated

   **C**   It is a worthwhile process

   **D**   Reviewers may be biased in their responses

10   Which one of the following is not a reason to provide a reference section in a practical report?

   **A**   To avoid being accused of plagiarism

   **B**   To acknowledge the source of the material used

   **C**   To make the report look better

   **D**   To allow the reader to be able to identify and access the sources cited

11   Which of the following is the correct Harvard referencing format?

   **A**   Milgram, S. (1963) Behavioural study of obedience. *Journal of Abnormal and Social Psychology*, 67, (4)

   **B**   Milgram, S. (1963) 'Behavioural study of obedience', *Journal of Abnormal and Social Psychology*, 67, (4), 371–378

   **C**   Milgram, S. (1963) *Behavioural study of obedience. Journal of Abnormal and Social Psychology*, 67, (4), 371–378

   **D**   Milgram, S. (1963) Behavioural study of obedience. Journal of Abnormal and Social Psychology, 67, (4), 371–378

12   Why is falsification an important element of the scientific method?

   **A**   Because it is easy

   **B**   Because it is hard

   **C**   Because falsifying hypotheses allows for scientific progress whereas confirming hypotheses does not

   **D**   Because falsifying hypotheses is proof

13 Which type of design is being used in an experiment to compare the reaction times of males and females?

A Repeated measures

C Independent measures

B Matched pairs

D Combined measures

14 Which test would you use to analyse interval, normally distributed data collected from an independent measures experiment?

A Mann–Whitney U-test

C Chi-squared test

B Unrelated t-test

D Related t-test

15 Which test would you use to analyse ordinal data collected from an independent measures experiment?

A Mann–Whitney U-test

C Chi-squared test

B Unrelated t-test

D Related t-test

16 Which test would you use to analyse interval, normally distributed data collected from a repeated measures experiment?

A Mann–Whitney U-test

C Chi-squared test

B Unrelated t-test

D Related t-test

17 Which of the following words refers to the ability to reproduce the procedure of an investigation?

A Validity

C Objectivity

B Falsifiability

D Replicability

18 Which of the following words refers to the process of refuting a hypothesis?

A Validity

C Objectivity

B Falsifiability

D Replicability

19 You have collected data on people's self-reported stress levels and the number of caffeine-based drinks they have on an average day. You want to display your results in a graph. Which graph is the most appropriate for these data?

A Scattergraph

C Pie chart

B Line graph

D Bar chart

20 You have collected data on how people travel to work: by car, bus, train, bike or walking. You want to display the results in a graph. Which graph is the most appropriate for these data?

A Scattergraph

C Pie chart

B Histogram

D Line graph

# ■ Section B

## Research design and response

### AS example 1

Total: 35 marks

A psychology teacher wishes to investigate whether her students are enjoying their AS psychology course. She decides to use a self-report method and to ask all the students who are in class on Monday morning.

**1** Suggest one open-ended question that could be used for this investigation. (2 marks)

*e* There is no one right answer for this question, but the examiners will be looking for a question that is clearly open ended (i.e. where the participants write their own answers rather than simply saying yes or no or choosing from a set of possible responses). They will also be looking for a question that is appropriate for this investigation. A question such as: 'Are you male/female?' *or* 'How old are you?' is unlikely to achieve any marks.

**2** Suggest one closed question that could be used for this investigation. (2 marks)

*e* This time you are being asked for a closed question. A clear and appropriate example will be awarded 2 marks, but this will need to include the response options as well as the question in order to make it clear that it is a closed question.

**3** Explain the difference between qualitative and quantitative data. (3 marks)

*e* Qualitative data are data that are collected in people's own words or are descriptive data reported by a researcher in an observation or a case study. It is not generally possible to reduce qualitative data to numbers although it may be possible to group responses together. Quantitative data, in contrast, are numerical data. This might be the numbers of yes/no responses in a questionnaire or it might be the time taken to complete something. Numerical data can be subjected to descriptive and inferential statistical testing.

**4** Outline one strength and one weakness of using a self-report method for this investigation. (6 marks)

*e* The question asks for a strength and a weakness for this investigation (i.e. students' enjoyment of their AS psychology course). 3 marks are available for each and are awarded as follows: 1 mark for simply identifying a relevant strength or weakness; 2 marks for giving some more explanation, for example why something is a strength or weakness; and 3 marks for an answer that clearly explains the strength or weakness and relates this to the investigation of students' enjoyment of AS psychology.

**5** Name the sampling method used in this investigation. (1 mark)

*e* The sampling method here is opportunity sampling as the teacher simply used the students who were present at the time she wanted to conduct her study.

**6 (a)** Suggest one problem with the sampling method used in this investigation. (2 marks)

ⓔ The general problem with opportunity sampling is that it tends to lack representativeness and generalisability. This question is asking you to suggest a problem in the context of this investigation so you need to do that to get full marks. For example, you could suggest that the people who are present on a Monday morning may not be a representative sample of the whole group and that given that the investigation is about enjoyment of the course, asking the questions when some people are not there may bias the results in favour of enjoyment.

**(b)** Outline one other sampling method that could be used in this investigation. (3 marks)

ⓔ You could suggest any other sampling method here. The most likely answer will be random sampling. Simply naming an alternative sampling method is not going to get you full marks — you need to outline how it could be used in this investigation.

**7** Outline how each of the following ethical considerations could have been dealt with in this study.

**(a)** Confidentiality (2 marks)

**(b)** Informed consent (2 marks)

**(c)** Protection of participant (2 marks)

ⓔ There are 2 marks for each of these ethical considerations and you are asked to outline how each one could be dealt with in this study. This suggests that the second mark will be for making your answer relevant to this study rather than simply answering about ethical considerations in general terms.

**8** You have been asked to carry out a follow-up study to investigate the differences in ability to pay attention between students who enjoy psychology and students who do not enjoy psychology. Explain how you would carry out an experiment to investigate if there is a difference or not. Justify your decisions as part of your explanation. (12 marks)

You must refer to:

■ field or laboratory experiments

■ the experimental design you would use

■ at least one control you would use

You should use your own experience of carrying out an experiment to inform your response.

ⓔ This question is worth 12 marks so you need to spend some time thinking about it. The exam paper is quite helpful as it gives you a list of some things that you must refer to — clearly this indicates that not referring to them would mean that you would not be able to achieve full marks. You have been told that the study is an experiment, and you have been told that the groups are students who enjoy psychology and students who do not enjoy psychology. This should tell you that you should be conducting an experiment with independent measures as clearly someone cannot be in both these groups. There are lots of things that could be controlled such as the type of task, previous experience with the task as well as general environmental variables. You need to explain in as much detail as you can exactly how this investigation would be conducted.

**Student A**

**1** 'What do you think of the sixth form?'

**e 1/2 marks awarded.** The question 'What do you think of the sixth form?' is not necessarily asking about students' enjoyment of their AS psychology course. However, it is not completely irrelevant and is clearly an open-ended question, so it scores 1 mark.

**2** 'Do you like psychology? Yes/No.'

**e 2/2 marks awarded.** This closed question is clear and appropriate.

**3** Quantitative data are data that are collected in numerical form. This could be the numbers of people that said yes or no to the question 'do you like psychology?' Quantitative data would also be data that were collected from rating scales where people rated their enjoyment on a 1–10 scale. Qualitative data are words not numbers.

**e 2/3 marks awarded.** This answer started well. Student A obviously understands what quantitative data are and has given some specific examples that relate to this study. The description of qualitative data is very brief, although it is correct to say 'not numbers'.

**4** The strength of using a self-report method for an investigation into students' enjoyment of A-level psychology is that you are asking them directly. The alternative would be to try to work out whether they enjoyed the classes from observing their behaviour and this might not be reliable. The weakness is that students might not tell the truth if they are asked by a teacher — they might respond to demand characteristics, for example thinking that they need to say yes they do enjoy the subject because they think this is what the teacher wants them to say. Some questions might be problematic because if people are given a choice of possible answers, the one they would have given might not be there and so the results become inaccurate.

**e 6/6 marks awarded.** This is an excellent answer. The strength and the weakness are well explained in the context of this observation.

**5** The sampling method is opportunity because the teacher is just using the people who are there at the time.

**e 1/1 mark awarded.** This is correct.

6 (a) One problem is that it does not really give you a representative sample because you are simply using the people who were there at the time. In this study there could have been lots of people not present at the time that the teacher asked them to complete this study and maybe the people who really like psychology are more likely to be there than the ones who do not like psychology.

*e* **2/2 marks awarded.** This is a good answer which identifies the general problem of a lack of representativeness as well as a more specific problem about this study.

(b) I would use a stratified sample of all the psychology students so that I had the correct proportions of males and females as well as correct proportions of ages and any other variables that might be important such as what other subjects people are doing along with psychology. This would give me a much more representative sample of the psychology students in the college.

*e* **3/3 marks awarded.** This is an interesting suggestion. Stratified sampling would provide a more representative sample and this has been well explained.

7 (a) It is important that information is confidential because otherwise students will not give their honest opinions. This could be done by ensuring that students did not have to write anything on the form that could lead to their handwriting being identified and putting the finished questionnaire in a sealed envelope. Alternatively they could do the questionnaire online with a number rather than a name.

*e* **2/2 marks awarded.** This is a good suggestion for dealing with this issue.

(b) No one should be taking part in any study without knowing exactly what they are taking part in. The teacher would need to explain exactly what the students need to do and what the data would be used for. The teacher would also have to make sure that the students knew that they did not have to take part and ensure that they did not feel any pressure to take part. They might because the teacher is asking them so perhaps she could get another student to give the questionnaires out.

*e* **2/2 marks awarded.** This is quite a lengthy answer but it does make a number of good suggestions.

(c) It is highly unlikely that taking part in this study would present any issues for any students but the teacher needs to make sure that she considers this. Perhaps people would be upset about being asked if they really did not like psychology and the teacher might have to consider how to deal with really negative responses.

**ⓔ 2/2 marks awarded.** This is a good answer again. Student A is right to say that there may not be any major protection issues in this study but is also right to say that the teacher needs to consider this carefully.

> **8**  I would use the data from this self-report to divide the students into two groups. The first group would be those who answered 'yes' to the question 'Do you like psychology?' and the second group would be those who answered 'no' to the same question. This would mean that I would have an independent measures design. I would base the experiment around something that the students were doing in class and would conduct the experiment in their own classroom so this would be a field experiment rather than a laboratory experiment. The independent variable is whether the students like psychology or not and the dependent variable is how much information they remember from an unexpected visit to the classroom. This would be another member of staff coming in to talk to the teacher and she would have some things with her (not books or things that might be guessed or really unexpected items that would definitely be remembered), such as a camera or an extension lead. At the end of the lesson the teacher would hand out a sheet of questions based on this event. The questions would be marked and the maximum total would be 10. The data could then be analysed using a Mann–Whitney test (independent measures and ordinal data).

**ⓔ 10/12 marks awarded.** This is a very detailed answer which explains clearly how to conduct this study. It even includes information about how these data would be analysed. However, the question does ask for the inclusion of at least one control and this has not been explicitly covered.

**ⓔ Total score: 33/35 marks. This is an excellent set of answers which demonstrate a very good understanding of research methods.**

| Student B |
| --- |

**1**  An open-ended question could be 'What do you like and what don't you like about AS psychology?'

**ⓔ 2/2 marks awarded.** This is an appropriate open-ended question.

**2**  A closed question could be 'Do you like psychology? Yes/No.'

**ⓔ 2/2 marks awarded.** This is an appropriate closed question.

**3**  Quantitative data are data in numbers and qualitative data are words and descriptions.

**ⓔ 2/3 marks awarded.** This is a good answer, but more explanation could have been included and an example of each type of data would have made this even clearer.

**4**   One strength of using a self-report method is that we are asking people directly rather than trying to interpret their behaviour. One weakness is that people may not tell the truth.

ⓔ **2/6 marks awarded.** These are appropriate responses, but check the question and the mark allocation. The candidate needs to describe a strength and a weakness for this specific investigation. The strength and weakness identified need to be described in more detail and the answer needs to relate to students' enjoyment of AS psychology.

**5**   This was an opportunity sample.

ⓔ **1/1 mark awarded.** As there is only 1 mark here, this is enough.

**6**   **(a)** One problem with an opportunity sample is that you are only using the people who are there at the time that you carry out the study and this might lead to a lack of representativeness.

ⓔ **1/2 marks awarded.** This would be a good answer to a question asking about the problems of opportunity samples in general, but this question asks specifically about this study. Student B needs to go a little further and explain this in the context of this investigation.

   **(b)** It might be better to have a random sample of all the psychology students in the whole college (or even in several colleges). This could be done by allocating everyone a number and drawing the numbers out of a hat (or using a random number table).

ⓔ **2/3 marks awarded.** This is a good answer which shows understanding of random sampling and makes some reference to the study. A little more detail is needed in order to achieve the third mark.

**7**   **(a)** It would be important to make sure that all the participants knew that their results would be kept confidential.

   **(b)** It would be important to make sure that all the participants gave informed consent.

   **(c)** It would be important to protect all the participants.

ⓔ **0/6 marks awarded.** There are 6 marks available in total here (2 for each part of the question). All that Student B has done is to repeat the terms identified in the question and say that it is important to make sure this is done. This will not achieve any marks. The examiners will be looking for suggestions about how, for example, participants could be protected. This demonstrates how important it is to read the question properly.

> **8** I would carry out a field experiment because I would do the experiment in the students' own classroom so it would be in the natural environment. I would show them a video with lots of things happening and tell them that they were going to be tested on what they remembered. I would ask questions about things that were not the main events in the video.

*e* **2/12 marks awarded.** Student B needed to give much more information for a question worth 12 marks. The examiners will be looking for enough detail to allow them to understand exactly how the suggested study would be conducted. There is plenty of time to think about this question and plan your answer before starting to write.

*e* **Total score: 14/35 marks. Most of the marks have been lost because not enough detail has been given in the answers or because the questions have not been read carefully enough.**

# AS example 2

Total: 35 marks

A researcher has conducted an experiment to see if people complete a simple task faster in the morning or the afternoon. The task was a jigsaw puzzle of 100 pieces and the participants attempted the puzzle in a room on their own. The time it took from starting the puzzle to finishing it was recorded. Participants were tested twice, once in the morning and once in the afternoon and a different 100-piece jigsaw was used for the morning and the afternoon test.

**1** Identify the independent and dependent variable in this experiment.　(2 marks)

*e* The question asks for two types of variable and each correct answer will gain 1 mark.

**2** Construct an appropriate null hypothesis for this investigation.　(3 marks)

*e* Remember that the null hypothesis is the 'no effect' hypothesis and so you should not be predicting any difference between performance in the morning and in the afternoon. You should also include both independent and dependent variables in this.

**3** Explain why the researcher chose to have the participants attempt the puzzle in a room on their own.　(4 marks)

*e* This is asking you to explain why the researcher made certain decisions about how to conduct the research. There are 4 marks available here and so the examiner will be looking for some detail and explanation. Simply identifying a reason why the researcher might have chosen to conduct the research in this way will get 1–2 marks, but a clear and detailed explanation will be expected for 3–4 marks. For full marks, the examiner will expect to see a well-explained answer that includes the use of appropriate terminology.

**4** Explain why the researcher used a different 100-piece jigsaw for the morning and the afternoon test. (4 marks)

ⓔ This is also asking you to consider why the researcher made certain decisions. As with the previous question, simply identifying a reason why the researcher might have chosen to conduct the research in this way will get 1–2 marks, but a clear and detailed explanation will be expected for 3–4 marks. For full marks, the examiner will expect to see a well-explained answer that includes the use of appropriate terminology.

**5 (a)** Name an appropriate measure of central tendency that could be used to summarise the data. (1 mark)

ⓔ The data are time so the most appropriate measure of central tendency is the mean. There is only 1 mark available here so just naming this will be enough.

**(b)** In which section of a report would this appear? (1 mark)

ⓔ This would appear in the results section. Again there is only 1 mark and so simply identifying this section will be enough.

**6 (a)** Explain what is meant by an extraneous variable. (2 marks)

ⓔ An extraneous variable is one that has not been controlled and so may be having an effect on the dependent variable. This question is asking for an explanation of this and 1 mark would be awarded for a brief explanation or for one that lacks clarity and 2 marks for a clear explanation.

**(b)** Identify one possible extraneous variable in this study. (2 marks)

ⓔ There are a number of extraneous variables in most pieces of research so it should not be too difficult to think of something. There is no mention of anything being controlled other than the fact that the participants completed the puzzle on their own. Although you do not have to go into much detail for this question, make sure that you make it clear what the variable is.

**(c)** Suggest one way in which this extraneous variable could be controlled. (2 marks)

ⓔ There are 2 marks available so you need to give a little bit of information but do not go into too much detail.

**7** Outline one ethical issue that would need to be considered in conducting this study. (2 marks)

ⓔ This study does not raise any serious ethical concerns but all studies should consider issues of informed consent, confidentiality and the right to withdraw even if the researchers are sure that their research will not raise any concerns over the protection of participants. You should identify the issue that you choose and explain its relevance in this study.

**8** You have been asked to carry out a follow-up study to investigate whether the same effects are found with a complex task in a real-life situation. Explain how you would carry out an experiment to investigate this. Justify your decisions as part of your explanation. (12 marks)

You must refer to:

- field, laboratory or quasi- experiments
- the experimental design you would use
- at least one control you would use

You should use your own experience of carrying out an experiment to inform your response.

🅔 This question is worth 12 marks so you need to spend some time thinking about it. The exam paper is quite helpful as it gives you a list of some things that you must refer to — clearly this indicates that not referring to them would mean that you would not be able to achieve full marks. You have been told that the study is an experiment and that you should be investigating this in a real-life situation. There are many things that could be controlled such as the type of task, previous experience with the task as well as general environmental variables. You need to explain in as much detail as you can exactly how this investigation would be conducted.

---

**Student A**

1   The independent variable is the time of day, either morning or afternoon. The dependent variable is the length of time it takes the participant to complete a 100-piece jigsaw.

🅔 **2/2 marks awarded.** This is correct and worth full marks.

2   The time of day will have no effect on the time that it takes the participant to complete a 100-piece jigsaw.

🅔 **3/3 marks awarded.** This is a clear and well-constructed null hypothesis with all the necessary information included.

3   Putting the participants in a room on their own has several advantages. First, they will not be able to see anyone else doing the same puzzle and so they will not be able to copy them. Second, they will not feel in competition with other people or stressed because they can see other people doing the puzzle faster than them. It also means that the conditions are the same for every participant, and this would be harder to control if there were more than one participant in the room.

🅔 **4/4 marks awarded.** This is an excellent answer.

**4** If the researcher had used the same puzzle twice people might complete it faster just because it was the second time that they had done it. They may remember something about doing it the first time that would help them. Alternatively, they may find doing the same puzzle again boring and take longer the second time as they cannot be bothered to do the same puzzle twice. Using a different puzzle reduces the first problem (although people might still be better generally when they do a puzzle for the second time) and it reduces the possible boredom created by doing the same puzzle twice. I think the researcher used a different puzzle because there would be fewer confounding variables than if he or she had used the same one twice.

*e* **4/4 marks awarded.** This is another excellent answer.

**5 (a)** The mean

*e* **1/1 mark awarded.**

**(b)** The results section.

*e* **1/1 mark awarded.**

**6 (a)** An extraneous variable is one that has not been controlled by the researcher and may potentially confound the dependent variable. This means that it may have an effect on the dependent variable so that it is difficult to determine whether it is the independent variable or the extraneous (uncontrolled variable) that is having the effect.

*e* **2/2 marks awarded.** This is a good answer. It is clear that Student A understands this concept very well indeed.

**(b)** One extraneous variable in this study might be to do with the environment in which people were tested. It might be that the room was warmer in the afternoon than in the morning or was sunnier in the morning than in the afternoon. This could be the variable that is responsible for the change in the dependent variable rather than the time of day.

*e* **2/2 marks awarded.** This is another good answer.

**(c)** This could be controlled by ensuring that the temperature and light levels were kept constant throughout the day.

*e* **2/2 marks awarded.** Although a brief answer this is enough to earn both marks.

**7** I would ensure that all the participants knew that they had the right to withdraw.

ⓔ **1/2 marks awarded.** To achieve the second mark, Student A needed to give this answer in the context of the study being discussed here.

> **8** I would choose a workplace where people have to grasp complex procedures quickly such as a factory that makes lots of different technological products. I would ask if it was possible for workers to be trained in two new procedures, one in the morning and one in the afternoon. I would try to control these as much as possible by ensuring that the two tasks had the same number of steps in them. I would time the first attempt to complete the procedure after training in the morning and again after training on the second procedure in the afternoon. If there were enough participants and the workplace allowed me I would counterbalance the tasks so that some people did task 1 in the morning and some people did task 2 in the morning. This would reduce any order effects. I could also ask someone else to time without the workers being aware of me watching because I might have an effect on them.

ⓔ **9/12 marks awarded.** This is a detailed answer which shows a good grasp of research methods. Unfortunately Student A has not addressed the issue of field/lab/quasi experiment in this answer and it might have been useful to give a little more information about the type of procedures that would be used.

ⓔ **Total score: 31/35 marks. This competent set of answers shows a good grasp of research methods and a careful reading of the questions.**

## Student B

> **1** The independent variable is the time of day and the dependent variable is the time it took them to complete the puzzle.

ⓔ **2/2 marks awarded.** This is correct, for full marks.

> **2** The time of day will have no effects.

ⓔ **1/3 marks awarded.** This answer is incomplete. A null hypothesis needs to contain information about both the independent and the dependent variable as well as the statement of 'no effect' or 'no difference'.

> **3** It is probably because they would not be able to copy anyone else.

ⓔ **1/4 marks awarded.** This is a reasonable suggestion for 1 mark, but the examiner is looking for more detail as this is a 4-mark question.

> **4** So that they did not remember how to do it.

ⓔ **1/4 marks awarded.** This is not enough for full marks. Ideally, you should include psychological terminology in your answer.

**5 (a)** Mean

*e* **1/1 mark awarded.**

**(b)** Results

*e* **1/1 mark awarded.**

**6 (a)** An extraneous variable is a confounding variable.

*e* **0/2 marks awarded.** The examiner will expect an explanation of what an extraneous variable is rather than just another piece of terminology. Although this is partially correct as an extraneous variable could be a potential confounding variable, there is not enough explanation in this answer to achieve any marks.

**(b)** If people like jigsaws.

*e* **1/2 marks awarded.** There is just enough information here for 1 mark. This is a reasonable suggestion although whether people are good at jigsaws or spend a lot of time doing jigsaws might have been a better suggestion. Even then, the fact that this is repeated measures might mean that this has been controlled for to an extent. It is the difference in performance that is being measured, not how good or bad someone is at jigsaws. Whichever variable was chosen, this answer needs to be expanded to include a brief explanation of why this is an extraneous variable (and perhaps the effect it might have).

**(c)** You could only use people who like jigsaws.

*e* **1/2 marks awarded.** This is another reasonable suggestion which would also score just 1 mark due to a lack of explanation.

**7** One ethical issue is consent. People should be allowed to withdraw.

*e* **0/2 marks awarded.** Student B has identified two different ethical issues but has not elaborated on either. This is not an outline of an issue that needs to be considered in this study and this would not achieve any marks.

**8** I would go to a factory where people were making complex things and I would watch them. I would time them doing their job in the morning and then I would time them doing their job in their afternoon. This would be a field experiment because it is taking place in people's real environment and it would be independent measures because I would control who was in the groups.

*e* **2/12 marks awarded.** This is a weak answer, containing some inaccuracies. There is a reasonable suggestion at the beginning where Student B suggests using a factory setting. However, by simply timing people in the morning and in the afternoon, there is no experimental manipulation going on and so this is not really a field experiment although it could be described as a quasi-experiment. It is not independent measures but repeated measures as the same people are taking part in each group.

*e* **Total score: 11/35 marks. It is important to give as much explanation and elaboration of answers as possible, especially when there are more than 1 or 2 marks available.**

# A-level example 1

Total: 35 marks

A researcher wishes to conduct an observation of students' food choices in a college canteen and to discover whether boys or girls choose healthier food.

**1**   Outline one strength and one weakness of using an observation for this
     investigation.                                                                                       (6 marks)

*e* There are 6 marks available and it is important that you take this into account when answering this question. There are several strengths and weaknesses that you could outline but you must choose ones that are directly relevant to this study. If you give general strengths and weaknesses of observation you will not achieve full marks.

**2**   Describe one ethical issue that the researcher needs to consider when
     conducting this observation and suggest how this could be dealt with.          (4 marks)

*e* You are asked to describe an ethical issue and to suggest how this issue could be dealt with. There are 2 marks for each part of the question. Simply identifying an issue will get you 1 mark, but describing it appropriately will get you 2 marks. Similarly, for the second part, if you make a brief or general suggestion, you will be awarded 1 mark, but if you explain your suggestion, you will gain 2 marks.

**3**   **(a)** Explain what is meant by 'inter-rater reliability'.                             (3 marks)

*e* A clear explanation of the term is expected for 3 marks. If your description has merit but is brief or could be clearer, it will only be awarded 1 or 2 marks.

   **(b)** Suggest how the researcher could ensure that this observation has inter-
        rater reliability.                                                                                   (4 marks)

*e* This requires a suggestion given in the context of the observation described in the question. If you simply outline a general suggestion for ensuring inter-rater reliability, you will only get a maximum of 2 marks, as the other 2 marks are awarded for focusing on the observation in the question. For example, if you discuss the categories specifically, this would be contextualising your answer, which is what the examiners are looking for.

You have been asked to carry out further observations to investigate the food choices of males and females in shopping centre food courts.

**4** Write an alternative hypothesis for your investigation. (3 marks)

**e** This is the experimental (rather than the null) hypothesis. It is important that you include both independent and dependent variables, as well as making it clear whether your hypothesis is directional or non-directional (one- or two-tailed).

**5** Explain how you would carry out an observation to investigate the food choices of males and females in shopping centre food courts. Justify your decisions as part of your explanation. (15 marks)

You must refer to:

- structured or unstructured observations
- participant or non-participant observations
- time or event sampling
- collection of data

You should use your own experience of carrying out an observation to inform your response.

**e** The question gives you a great deal of information and you need to read it carefully. You have been told what you are observing (although you will need to outline the categories that you will use if you are conducting a structured observation) and you have been told where you are observing. If you follow the guidance in the points after 'You must refer to', then you will be giving the examiners the material that they are looking for.

### Student A

**1** One strength of an observation is that it has high ecological validity if it is conducted in a natural environment and participants are unaware of being observed. This should apply here as it should be relatively easy to observe food choices in a school canteen without drawing attention to the fact that people are being observed (which might risk them changing their behaviour). One weakness of an observation like this is that there is little control. There may be lots of variables affecting food choice that the researcher is unaware of and is not able to control.

**e** **5/6 marks awarded.** This is a good answer although it could be argued that the strength is better explained than the weakness. Including an example of a variable that has not been controlled would help to improve the description of the weakness.

**2** One ethical issue is consent. In most psychological research it is essential that participants give their fully informed consent before starting the research. However, it is permissible to conduct observational research in a public place without permission from participants. I would not have to ask for permission to conduct this observation as it would be considered a public place and I am not collecting any personal information from the participants, such as their names or any health information. This is an advantage as people would not be tempted to buy a healthier lunch because they knew that they were being observed.

*ⓔ* **4/4 marks awarded.** The issue of consent has been identified and described. The student explains how this issue relates to observational research and has linked it to the observation described. This answer achieves full marks despite wandering off the point a little at the end with talk about issues of social desirability.

3  **(a)** Inter-rater reliability means that two or more observers record the same information when observing the same behaviours.

*ⓔ* **3/3 marks awarded.** This explanation is exactly right.

**(b)** The researcher could ensure that this observation has inter-rater reliability by compiling the observation sheet in such a way that all the observer has to do is record the food on the tray. The lead researcher would categorise the food as healthy or unhealthy, so there is no room for the observers to have to make this judgement. This is where levels of inter-rater reliability may fall because different observers may judge certain foods differently. The researcher would also need to train the observers to use the observation sheet before they conducted the real observation.

*ⓔ* **4/4 marks awarded.** This is a good answer. Student A has suggested that the more objective the coding becomes, the more likely it is that two or more observers will agree. So if observers only have to tick exactly what each person buys, there is less room for individual differences of opinion than there might be if the observers had to decide whether someone's lunch was healthy or unhealthy. The student also mentions training the observers, which would also reduce differences of interpretation.

4  There will be a difference in the food choices of males and females eating in a shopping centre food court.

*ⓔ* **3/3 marks awarded.** This is a clear alternate hypothesis which contains details of the independent variable (male/female) and the dependent variable (food choices). This is a non-directional hypothesis as it does not state which direction the difference will be (males or females healthier for example).

5  I would conduct this as a structured observation and I would design a coding sheet with categories for all the different food outlets. I would decide if they were healthy or unhealthy. I would make this a participant observation as I would buy some food and sit near the food counter to observe. I would count how many males and females went to each counter. I would do this for an hour in the morning, an hour at lunchtime and another hour in the afternoon.

*ⓔ* **4/15 marks awarded.** Student A has not spent very much time on this question and so does not earn many marks. There should be plenty of time to think carefully and to plan your answer in detail.

Ⓔ **Total score: 23/35 marks. Many of these marks were lost on the final question. It is important to take into account the mark allocations for each question when judging how much to write.**

> **Student B**
>
> **1**  Observations are not very reliable but they are quite easy and cheap to set up.

Ⓔ **0/6 marks awarded.** This answer would not achieve any marks. These are not only very general points with no relevance to this specific observation but they are much too vague. The weakness that has been selected (lack of reliability) needs to be explained and the strength is not worth any credit at all.

> **2**  I would have to ask for permission from everyone who was going to take part.

Ⓔ **1/4 marks awarded.** The ethical issue has not been identified to begin with and, although the reader can assume that the issue is consent, it has not been clearly explained. The issue of consent is slightly different when considering observational research and it is not always necessary to ask for consent if an observation is in a public place. This answer only gains 1 (generous) mark for a weak attempt at dealing with an unidentified issue.

> **3**  **(a)**  Inter-rater reliability is how consistent the results are.

Ⓔ **1/3 marks awarded.** This is not quite right and only achieves 1 mark. Inter-rater reliability is how consistently different observers make judgements or record information and is more about measurement than results.

> **(b)**  Inter-rater reliability can be measured by correlating the scores from two observers to see how much they agree with each other.

Ⓔ **2/4 marks awarded.** Yes, this is how inter-rater reliability can be measured, but the question asks for more than this. What if the researcher measured inter-rater reliability and found that it was poor — what would they have to do then? This answer is only awarded 2 marks as it needs to include some suggestion about what to do to ensure that the observers agree with each other.

> **4**  There will be no difference in the food choices of males and females.

Ⓔ **0/3 marks awarded.** This is a null hypothesis not an alternate hypothesis so would not achieve any marks.

**5** I would use this and I would observe all day in the food court.

| | Male | Female |
|---|---|---|
| Healthy | | |
| Unhealthy | | |

*e* **2/15 marks awarded.** Student B needs to read the question and think carefully about what they have been asked to do. All the pointers in the question need to be addressed and full details of how the observation would be conducted need to be included.

*e* **Total score: 6/35 marks. Remember to check the number of marks available for each question and plan your time accordingly.**

# A-level example 2

Total: 35 marks

**You have been asked to design a piece of research to investigate parents' use of physical punishment. You have decided to use a self-report method.**

**1** Suggest how you might obtain an appropriate sample of participants for this study. (3 marks)

*e* The question asks for a suggestion. There are 3 marks available, so simply identifying a sampling technique will only get you 1 mark. You are expected to give more detail about where and how the sample might be obtained. You will be awarded 2 marks for identifying a sampling technique and giving some information, such as 'an opportunity sample from a school'. Increasing the amount of detail you give will increase the marks you achieve. For 3 marks, the examiner will be looking for a detailed suggestion about how the sample would be obtained.

**2** Outline two ethical issues that you would need to consider and how you would deal with these. (8 marks)

*e* There are 2 marks for each issue you outline. Just identifying an ethical issue will get you 1 mark, but giving some detail about the issue (preferably in the context of this investigation) will get you 2 marks. Similarly, identifying a way of dealing with each issue and explaining this in more detail will achieve the full 2 marks for each.

**3 (a)** Outline two methodological problems that you might encounter when conducting this research. (4 marks)

*e* As with question 2, there are 2 marks for each methodological problem you outline. Identifying a problem will get you 1 mark and expanding on this answer, possibly by explaining why you might encounter this problem, will get you the second mark.

**(b)** Suggest what effect one of these problems might have on the results of this study. (2 marks)

*e* This could be answered by considering one effect of the problem you select in detail, or by considering more effects in less detail. 1 mark will be given for identifying an effect and a further mark will be given for some elaboration that makes reference to the results.

**You have been asked to carry out a further study using self-report measures to investigate the use of physical punishment by parents in different countries.**

**4** Write a null hypothesis for your investigation. (3 marks)

*e* You are being asked for the null hypothesis here. This is the 'no effect' or 'no difference' hypothesis so it important to use one of these phrases in your hypothesis. You should also include both the independent and dependent variables.

**5** Explain how you would carry out the investigation into the use of physical punishment by parents in different countries. Justify your decisions as part of your explanation. You must refer to: (15 marks)

- questionnaires or interviews (structured/semi-structured/unstructured)
- open and closed questions
- rating scales
- collection of data

You should use your own experience of carrying out a self-report to inform your response.

*e* The question gives you a huge amount of guidance. You know that you have to design something which compares two (or more) countries. You know that you have to use a self-report measure and that the questions need to be about the use of physical punishment. Follow the guidance points carefully to make sure that you include everything that the examiner is looking for.

### Student A

**1** I would use a volunteer sampling method in a school. I would ask the head teacher to send a letter home to all the parents asking them if they would take part. I would try to get 20 parents to complete the questionnaire.

*e* **2/3 marks awarded.** A volunteer sample is appropriate and the student has given some information about how this would be achieved. However, more detail could have been given, for example, would the questionnaires have been sent home with the letters or would people simply have been told what the questions would be about?

**2** One ethical issue is informed consent. Participants should always be told what the research is about and should be able to make an informed decision about whether to participate. I would tell them in the letter that they would be asked about their use of physical punishment and then they could decide if they wanted to take part. Another ethical issue is confidentiality. Participants have the right to know that their data are being kept confidential and that no one would be able to identify them from their answers. I would deal with this by telling them in the letter that they could complete the questionnaire at home and would not have to put their name on it. I would also ensure that I did not include questions that asked for any information that could be used to identify the parents or their children.

**ℯ 8/8 marks awarded.** Two appropriate ethical issues have been identified and outlined in the context of this investigation. The suggestions for dealing with these issues are also explained well.

3 **(a)** One methodological problem is that parents might lie in response to some of the questions about physical punishment due to social desirability bias. This means they might not want to admit that they smack their children because they might think that this makes them a bad parent. Therefore, the results would not be a true picture of the behaviour of the participants as it would suggest that few if any parents use physical punishment and the results would not be valid. Another problem would be getting a representative sample of parents. Parents who use physical punishment might refuse to take part in the study as they might think they are going to be judged. Therefore, parents who do not use physical punishment might be over-represented in the sample. This would again mean that we are not getting a true picture of what sort of physical punishment is being used by parents and how widespread it is.

**ℯ 4/4 marks awarded.** This is a very good answer and is worth full marks. However, it is worth noting that Student A has answered part b as well as part a. Although there will be no penalty for doing this, it does waste time and Student A is going to have to write part of this answer out again in part b as the examiner will not credit material across questions.

**(b)** The effect of the social desirability bias would mean that the researcher would probably not get a true picture of the use of physical punishments as most parents would not admit to using it even if they did. This would probably make the results invalid.

**ℯ 2/2 marks awarded.** This is another good answer which shows a good grasp of these concepts.

4 The null hypothesis would predict that there would be no difference in the use of physical punishment by parents in different countries. It would be worded something like: 'There will be no difference in the use of physical punishment by parents in the UK and parents in China.'

ⓔ **3/3 marks awarded.** This is a clear, well-constructed null hypothesis. The first sentence is not strictly necessary but does make it clear that Student A understands this.

> **5** This would be a cross-cultural study comparing the use of physical punishment by parents in two different countries: the UK and China. I have chosen these because they are very different cultures and because the one-child policy in China may have a significant effect on the way parents treat their children and the way that children behave if they are generally only children. I would use questionnaires rather than interviews as this would allow me to collect more data although I could consider a follow-up study where a smaller number of people were interviewed in depth. Perhaps my questionnaire would be a type of pilot study allowing me to identify any differences which could then be explored in more detail in the interviews. My questionnaires would need to be fairly short and easy to complete as I am going to use SurveyMonkey and obtain my participants through social media such as Facebook.
>
> I would ask parents of children under 18 to answer one questionnaire and I would have a second questionnaire for young people (16–18) to answer about their parents' use of physical punishment while they were growing up. I would not ask children any younger than that as this might create ethical issues although I would have to ensure that there was some kind of screening on the questionnaire to ensure that participants were old enough to answer. It would be good to get both parents' and children's opinions on the use of physical punishment by the parents as it would then be possible to see if the answers agreed (in general). I would have mostly closed questions on my questionnaire such as how often did your parents/you use physical punishment (and give a choice of answers) and what sort of physical punishment did you/your parents use (again with a choice of answers). I could have an open question at the end to allow people to write any further information but this would be difficult to analyse.

ⓔ **12/15 marks awarded.** This is a very thoughtful answer with good attention paid to the instruction to 'justify your decisions'. This is an interesting and well-thought out study, although the issue of age does lack a little bit of clarity. Overall though this is a very good answer.

ⓔ **Total score: 31/35 marks. These are thoughtful and well-presented answers.**

> **Student B**
>
> **1** Opportunity sampling — this is where you use whoever is around at the time and place you conduct the study.

ⓔ **1/4 marks awarded.** The question asks for a suggestion about how to obtain a sample for this particular study. Identifying 'opportunity sampling' is credited, but there are no further marks for the definition of opportunity sampling given here.

> 2   Consent and distress. Everyone would have to give consent to take part and I would not ask any questions that might distress people.

*e* **3/8 marks awarded.** This is a brief answer, but does provide some creditworthy material. 1 mark is given for consent and 2 marks for distress and the suggestion to avoid questions that might cause distress. However, there are 8 marks available here and the student needed to provide a much fuller discussion.

> 3   (a) Questions could be ambiguous and this might make the results wrong.

*e* **1/4 marks awarded.** There are 4 marks on offer here and the student has written 11 words. The first point is true — questions are often ambiguous and this is an important issue when conducting self-reports. However, more detail needs to be given, such as an example or a better description of the effect of asking ambiguous questions. The use of the word 'wrong' in relation to results is also too vague. Lastly, the question asks for two problems, so the student has already lost half the marks by only suggesting one.

> (b)  The results would be wrong.

*e* **0/2 marks awarded.** This would not achieve any marks. 'Wrong' is simply too vague a concept in this context. If Student B had discussed issues of validity this could have been a good answer.

> 4   There will be no difference in the physical punishment.

*e* **1/3 marks awarded.** This does not contain all the necessary information. There is no mention of the different countries (or of the parents).

> 5   I would interview parents about their use of physical punishment because they are less likely to lie if they are questioned face to face than if they are just filling in a questionnaire. I would ask 10 parents from one country and 10 parents from a different country and I would interview them in their homes. I would use a structured interview so I would know what questions to ask.

*e* **3/15 marks awarded.** This is far too brief to achieve more than 3 marks. What is here is quite chatty and the justifications are not always very good — for example, why might people be less likely to lie because they are being questioned face to face? How is the interviewer going to interview people in their homes if they are in different countries (or are they all in this country but came originally from other countries?) There are too many unanswered questions here.

*e* **Total score: 9/35 marks. The answers are brief and lacking explanation. There is plenty of time in the examination to provide more detail than this.**

# ■ Section C

## Data analysis and interpretation

### AS example 1

Total: 25 marks

A researcher has conducted an experiment to see if people recall more information when they learn and recall in a warm room rather than if they learn and recall in a cold room. This was an independent measures design. Participants all worked in a large hospital and were asked to go to either room 1 (warm) or room 2 (cold) when they had a few minutes free. Once in the room, participants had to read a complex passage relating to new equality legislation in the workplace and then were tested using an online multiple-choice test of ten questions.

The results are shown in the table.

| Condition A: learn and recall in a warm room | | Condition B: learn and recall in a cold room | |
|---|---|---|---|
| Participant | Score | Participant | Score |
| 1 | 7 | 1 | 8 |
| 2 | 7 | 2 | 8 |
| 3 | 6 | 3 | 8 |
| 4 | 9 | 4 | 9 |
| 5 | 5 | 5 | 6 |
| 6 | 8 | 6 | 8 |
| 7 | 5 | 7 | 7 |
| 8 | 4 | 8 | 6 |
| 9 | 5 | 9 | 8 |
| 10 | 7 | 10 | 9 |
| Total | 63 | Total | 77 |
| Mean | 6.3 | Mean | 7.7 |

**1** Outline how a mean is calculated. (2 marks)

ⓔ You will need to explain briefly the procedure to follow to work out a mean. The arithmetic mean is the average that is calculated by adding up all the scores in one condition and then dividing by the number of scores.

**2** Outline how a median is calculated. (2 marks)

ⓔ You will need to do the same for this question. The median is another measure of central tendency which is calculated by putting all the scores in one condition into rank order from lowest to highest and then choosing the mid-point from this list (either the central number or the mid-point between two numbers if there is an even number of numbers).

**3**  Calculate the median score for Condition A and Condition B. (2 marks)

*e* Make sure you say which median refers to which condition rather than just writing down two numbers.

**4**  Outline one conclusion that can be drawn from the above table. Refer to either the mean or the median scores in your answer. (2 marks)

*e* This is a good example of a question that needs to be read carefully. If you just skim read this question you might give a valid conclusion, but you might miss the requirement to refer to the mean or the median scores. You would not be able to achieve full marks without this. Remember too that you must give a conclusion rather than just restating the results.

**5**  Sketch an appropriate graph summarising the data. (4 marks)

*e* The most appropriate graph for this type of data would be a bar chart displaying the mean or the median. The question clearly says 'summarising the data' so it would not be appropriate to produce a graph of the raw data. Do not worry about the fact that you have no graph paper; the question clearly says 'sketch' so a freehand graph is fine. However, remember to label the axes of your graph and to give the graph a title. You will lose nearly all the marks without these.

**6**  The researcher used an independent measures design for this experiment.

  **(a)** Explain what an independent measures design is (2 marks)

*e* An independent measures design is where participants take part in only one condition of the experiment. In this study, this would mean that they would be in the 'warm' condition or the 'cold' condition but not both.

  **(b)** Explain why an independent measures design is a better choice than a repeated measures design for this study. (3 marks)

*e* You need to think about this carefully. There are strengths and weaknesses whichever design is selected, but why do you think that the researcher might have chosen to use an independent measures design for this study? It is likely to be because the weaknesses of an alternative (repeated measures) may have been greater than the weaknesses of using the independent measures design. For example, the independent measures design allows you to use the same material in both conditions although the weakness is that you have different people in each condition which could mean that participant variables are an issue. On the other hand, using the repeated measures design would remove the participant variables but you would not be able to use the same material in each condition and this might be a bigger problem.

**7**  Explain the purpose of peer review. (3 marks)

*e* The purpose of peer review is to ensure that research published in prestigious academic journals is of a high quality and is valid and unbiased. By sending submitted articles to other academics working in similar areas, the journal editors ensure that everything that is published is of the highest quality. Note that this question is asking you about the purpose of peer review rather than asking you to describe the process of peer review.

**8** Following a peer review of this study, the following comment was made: 'participant variables were insufficiently controlled'.

Suggest what this statement may mean in relation to this study. (5 marks)

ⓔ The first thing to note about this question is the mark allocation. When there are 5 marks available for a question it is important to expand your answer beyond a single point or a single sentence. The question gives you quite a lot of information to help construct your answer. You have been told that the issue is to do with participant variables which should lead you to think about the fact that there were different people in each condition of this investigation. This means that the difference in recall could have been due to participant variables rather than the manipulation of the independent variable. You need to consider what this means in terms of weaknesses of the study and you could also consider and discuss possible solutions to this.

---

**Student A**

**1** To calculate a mean, you need to add up all the scores and then divide by the number of scores that you have.

ⓔ **2/2 marks awarded.** Compare this answer to the one that Student B gives and you will see that Student A has given a much clearer explanation of how a mean is calculated.

---

**2** The median is calculated by putting all the scores into rank order and the median is the mid-point of this list. In this list there are ten scores so the median will be halfway between the 5th and 6th score.

ⓔ **2/2 marks awarded.** This is a clear explanation of how to calculate a median.

---

**3** The median for condition A is 6.5 and the median for condition B is 8.

ⓔ **2/2 marks awarded.** This is the correct answer for both and the candidate has helpfully told the examiner which score is for which condition.

---

**4** The group of participants learning and recalling in a cold room had a higher mean score of correct answers on the multiple-choice test (mean = 7.3) than the group of participants who completed the same tasks in a warm room (mean = 6.3).

ⓔ **2/2 marks awarded.** This is excellent. Not only has Student A explained one conclusion very clearly she has also referred to the means as instructed.

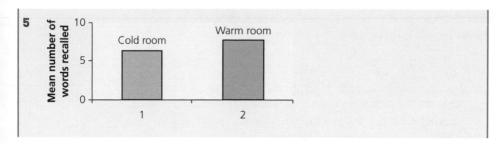

**5**

**ⓔ 3/4 marks awarded.** This is an appropriate graph which has been well labelled. If you compare this graph with the one in Student B's answer below, hopefully you can see that this makes more sense. However, this could still usefully have a caption. 'The mean number of words recalled by participants studying in either a cold room or a warm room' would be ideal. Due to the lack of a title, this graph would be worth 3 marks out of a possible 4.

**6 (a)** An independent measures design uses a different group of participants in each condition of the experiment. No participant should be exposed to more than one condition.

**ⓔ 2/2 marks awarded.** This is a clear explanation of an independent measures design. The second sentence makes it absolutely clear that Student A understands what an independent measures design is.

**(b)** This study used material on equality legislation. It would be impossible for people to be in both conditions and to be exposed to the same material twice as they would already know it. This would mean that if a repeated measures design were to be used different material would be required, and this would be a more serious confounding variable than any weakness of independent measures because any difference in recall could then be due to one set of information being easier to recall than the other set, rather than anything to do with the temperature of the room.

**ⓔ 3/3 marks awarded.** This is an excellent answer which demonstrates that Student A has a sophisticated understanding of the strengths and weaknesses of different experimental designs. It is clear that she understands that whichever design is chosen, there will be weaknesses to consider and she has explained that the weaknesses of an independent measures design are probably less significant in this study than the weaknesses of any other design would be.

**7** Before a report is published in an academic journal, it is sent to several other academics working in similar fields. They are asked to review the work before a decision is made about whether to publish. The purpose of this to ensure that high standards of research (both ethically and methodologically) are maintained.

**ℯ 3/3 marks awarded.** This is another good answer. A good understanding of both the how and the why of peer review is given here.

**8** There are a number of uncontrolled participant variables in this study. To begin with, the source simply tells us that the participants all worked in a large hospital. This means that there could have been a very wide range of roles and perhaps one group had more doctors and the other group more admin staff. This might have had an influence on how well they performed on the task and this may explain the difference in performance rather than the temperature of the room.

There is also no mention of controlling for previous knowledge of the equality legislation. It may be that several members of Condition B already knew some of the material that they were to be tested on, again this would explain why this group had the higher mean scores, Finally, the source tells us that participants were asked to go to one of the testing rooms 'when they had a few minutes' and this could have resulted in people being in very different states of minds due to whatever they were doing previously.

**ℯ 5/5 marks awarded.** There is a huge amount of information in this answer and Student A obviously understands the importance of the statement. There is also a very clear focus on this investigation rather than just discussing participant variables in general terms.

**ℯ Total score: 24/25 marks. This is an excellent set of answers and Student A only missed full marks by failing to put a title on the graph.**

### Student B

**1** A mean is an average.

**ℯ 1/2 marks awarded.** This does not give enough information — mean, median and mode are all averages. A better answer would be to say that the mean is the arithmetic average and is calculated by adding up all the scores and dividing by the number of scores. If in doubt give a little bit more information.

**2** A median is the middle number.

**ℯ 1/2 marks awarded.** Again, this does not go quite far enough. The median is the middle number when all the scores in the same condition are put in order from lowest to highest.

**3** 6.5 and 8.

**ℯ 1/2 marks awarded.** These figures are correct but Student B has not identified which one is which. This could well lose a mark in the examination.

**4**   People get more questions right in the cold room.

ⓔ **1/2 marks awarded.** This is broadly correct although some of the scores in the warm room are higher than some of the scores in the cold room. What would be more accurate would be to say that the average (mean or median) score in the cold room is higher than the mean/median in the warm room. If you included the mean or median scores you would also get the second mark as you would have fulfilled the second requirement of the question which explicitly asked you to refer to the mean or median. Make sure that you read the question carefully and attempt to do all that you are asked to do.

**5**
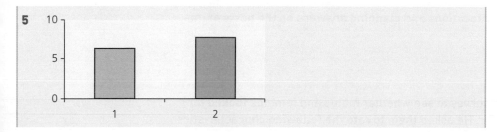

ⓔ **1/4 marks awarded.** There is no indication of what either axis is showing, there is no title telling the reader what the graph is displaying and it is not clear what 1 and 2 refer to.

**6**   **(a)** An independent measures design is where different people take part in each condition of the study.

ⓔ **2/2 marks awarded.** There is just enough for 2 marks here.

**(b)** Because they could not take part in both conditions.

ⓔ **0/3 marks awarded.** This answer is not clear enough. Why could people not take part in both conditions? Student B is on the right lines as clearly you could not ask someone to learn the same material twice (once in a cold room and once in a warm room) but this has not been explained well enough to achieve any marks.

**7**   Peer review is the process of reviewing work before it is published.

ⓔ **1/3 marks awarded.** It is really important that you look at the mark allocations for each question and judge how much information is required. Here Student B could have explained more about how and why the process of peer review is followed.

**8**   This might mean that there are characteristics of the participants that might explain the results and these have not been controlled by the researchers.

**ⓔ 1/5 marks awarded.** This is the start of a good answer although Student B needs to develop this much further to achieve more than 1 mark out of a possible 5. Although what he has written is broadly correct, it is little more than a rewriting of the information that is in the question. The examiners will be looking for a lot more information than this. For example, you could suggest which characteristics have not been controlled and perhaps even how they might have been controlled. You could also look at this in slightly wider terms — if there are variables that have not been controlled then perhaps the overall conclusions of the study are less valid and need to be questioned?

**ⓔ Total score: 9/25 marks. This is largely due to giving very brief answers which could have easily been elaborated. This low total may also be due to not taking notice of the mark allocations and planning answers on the basis of this.**

# AS example 2

Total: 25 marks

A researcher conducted a survey to see whether males and females looked for the same things in a partner. He asked them to rate the following characteristics on a scale from 1–10, where 1 is 'not important to me at all' and 10 is 'extremely important'.

- Physical attractiveness
- Intelligence
- Wealth
- Kindness
- Sense of humour

The researcher used an opportunity sample of 20 sixth-form students (10 male and 10 female) from a large city in the UK. The results are shown in the table.

| Characteristics | Mean rating | |
|---|---|---|
| | Males | Females |
| Physical attractiveness | 6.5 | 5 |
| Intelligence | 5 | 7 |
| Wealth | 5.2 | 5.9 |
| Kindness | 6.9 | 8.5 |
| Sense of humour | 4.3 | 5.8 |

**1 Outline two conclusions that could be drawn from the table.** (4 marks)

**ⓔ** You are asked for two conclusions and there are 4 marks available. A clear and accurate conclusion will be awarded 2 marks. A conclusion that is vague or lacks clarity will only gain 1 mark. A common mistake is for candidates to give an answer such as: 'Females give a higher rating for kindness'. This is incomplete as it is not clear whether females give a higher rating for kindness than they do for some other variable, or whether females give a higher rating for kindness than males do.

**2** The researchers have used a mean to describe their results. Suggest one other descriptive statistic that could be used and how this would be calculated. (3 marks)

*e* The most likely responses to this question would be to suggest a median or a mode. You would be awarded 1 mark for identifying an appropriate alternative and the other 2 marks would be awarded for the clarity of your description of how to calculate this. Remember that the median is the mid-point of all the scores when they are placed in rank order and the mode is the most common or most frequent response.

**3** Sketch a fully labelled bar chart displaying the results for any one characteristic. (4 marks)

*e* You are asked to sketch a fully labelled bar chart for any one characteristic. This means you can choose the characteristic and your bar chart should simply have two bars — one representing the average rating given by males and the other representing the average rating given by females. Just sketching the two bars without any labels will get you 1 mark. 2 marks will be awarded for an appropriate bar chart with some labelling, and 3 marks will be given for an appropriate bar chart with most of the labelling (or just minor omissions). For 4 marks, the examiner will expect to see clear and appropriate labelling with no omissions.

**4 (a)** Suggest one problem with the way that the sample for this study was selected. (2 marks)

*e* This question asks for just one problem and there are 2 marks available. Simply identifying a problem will be enough for 1 mark, but you will need to give more detail (ideally in the context of this sample and this study) to be awarded 2 marks.

**(b)** Suggest an alternative sampling technique and explain how this could have been used in this study. (3 marks)

*e* You could suggest any sampling techniques other than the one that has been used for this study. Probably the most obvious answer here would be to suggest a random sample. It will not be enough to simply identify this though — you will need to explain how a random sample could be acquired in this study.

**5** The researcher used a 1–10 rating scale to collect these data.
**(a)** Suggest one strength of using this type of rating scale in this study. (2 marks)
**(b)** Suggest one limitation of using this type of rating scale in this study. (2 marks)

*e* The examiners are expecting you to be aware of both the strengths and limitations of the different ways of collecting data. Rating scales have both strengths and limitations and you have a number to choose from. The crucial part of this question is the final few words 'in this study'. Whichever strength or weakness you select, make sure that you describe it in the context of this study.

**6** The researcher decides to make suggestions for future research in the final report. In which section of the report would this information go? (1 mark)

*e* This is a fairly straightforward question with just 1 mark available. The correct answer here is that any consideration of future research would be included in the discussion.

**7** **Suggest one improvement that the researcher might consider and outline the effect this might have on the results.** (4 marks)

*e* This question asks you to suggest any possible improvement. This gives you scope to consider the rating scales, sample or any other aspect of the investigation and to then discuss the effect that this might have on your results. There are 4 marks available and it is likely that a brief suggestion will only be awarded 1 mark, possibly increasing to 2 for a detailed suggestion and the rest of the marks will be awarded for the consideration of the effect that this might have on the results.

> ### Student A
>
> **1** Males rated physical attractiveness as more important in a partner than females did. Females rated wealth as more important in a partner than males did.

*e* **4/4 marks awarded.** Two clearly stated conclusions, for full marks.

> **2** I would have used a median or a mode. The median is calculated by putting all the scores in one condition in rank order (from highest to lowest) and then taking the middle number (or the mid-point if there is an even number of numbers). The mode is the most frequently given response.

*e* **3/3 marks awarded.** This would get full marks although Student A has wasted a little time here by giving two answers when only one was required.

**3**

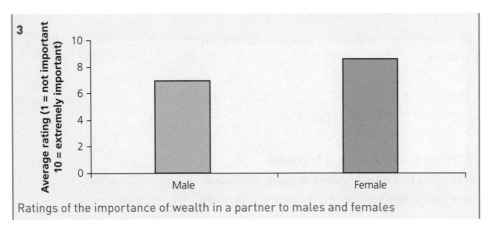

Ratings of the importance of wealth in a partner to males and females

*e* **4/4 marks awarded.** This bar chart gains full marks. The student has chosen one characteristic and has produced a fully labelled bar chart.

> **4** **(a)** The sample is too small. It is not possible to draw generalised conclusions about how males and females rate these characteristics when you have asked only 10 males and 10 females. The sample is also all students, which means it is not possible to generalise the results beyond students to a wider population.

**e 0/2 marks awarded.** Although the points given in this answer are all valid ones, they are not relevant to the question that was asked. The question clearly asks for problems with the way that the sample was selected rather than problems with the sample. This is another example of the importance of reading the question carefully.

> **(b)** This study needs a much larger and a much wider sample. I would suggest a sample of around 200 males and 200 females. This would have to be a stratified sample, representing different age groups, cultures and occupations. It could also include an equal number of people who have long-term partners and those who do not. This would mean the results could be generalised to a much wider population and might give a more accurate picture of the characteristics valued by males and females. This would make the results more useful.

**e 1/3 marks awarded.** Student A has suggested exactly who would be in the sample and has discussed the effect of using this improved sample, although there is no information about how this sample would be achieved.

> **5 (a)** They are fairly simple for people to complete and they produce data that can be easily compared.

**e 1/2 marks awarded.** There are two answers here and the question only asks for one. The second point is probably the strongest and would achieve 1 mark.

> **(b)** People may not all mean the same thing by the number they choose and so this may make comparisons less valid.

**e 2/2 marks awarded.** This is an interesting points and although it could be explained a little further, there is just enough here for 2 marks.

> **6** In the conclusion.

**e 0/1 mark awarded.** This is incorrect. Consideration of areas of future research would be in the discussion. You would never introduce new material in the conclusion which should simply be a restating of the main conclusions which have already been discussed.

> **7** I would use a much bigger sample of older people and of people from all over the world. I would suggest a sample of around 200 males and 200 females. This would have to be a stratified sample, representing different age groups, cultures and occupations. It could also include an equal number of people who have long-term partners and those who do not. This would mean the results could be generalised to a much wider population and might give a more accurate picture of the characteristics valued by males and females. This would make the results more useful.

ⓔ **4/4 marks awarded.** This is interesting. Student A has repeated his answer to an earlier question but this time the answer is entirely appropriate and would achieve 4/4 marks. If the student realised that the material was in the wrong place it was a good idea to repeat it here as the examiner will not give you credit in one question for material that you included in the answer to a different question.

ⓔ **Total score: 19/25 marks. There are some very good answers here but also some examples of losing marks by not reading the questions properly.**

> **Student B**
>
> **1** Males think that physical attractiveness is more important. Females think that wealth is slightly more important.

ⓔ **2/4 marks awarded.** Student B has given two conclusions, but both lack clarity. The first conclusion should say: 'Males think that physical attractiveness is more important in a partner than females do.' Otherwise, the conclusion given could be saying that males think that physical attractiveness is more important than intelligence. These conclusions are awarded 1 mark each.

> **2** They could have used a median.

ⓔ **1/3 marks awarded.** This is not enough for 3 marks. Median is a correct suggestion so 1 mark is awarded for this, but Student B has missed the second requirement of the question which was to explain how this would be calculated.

**3**

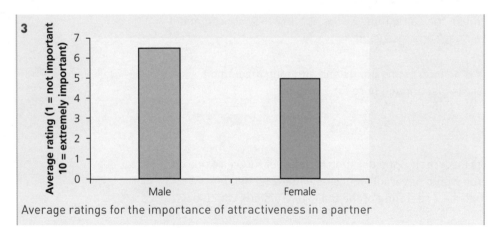

Average ratings for the importance of attractiveness in a partner

ⓔ **4/4 marks awarded.** This bar chart gains full marks. Student B has selected just one characteristic and has produced a clear chart with all the correct labelling.

> **4 (a)** One problem is that it was an opportunity sample from one school. This means that it will not be representative of people in other schools, those that left school or those that live in very different parts of the UK.

*e* **1/2 marks awarded.** This is a good answer although there is still room to expand this by explaining why this would not produce a representative sample.

> **(b)** You could have used a random sample.

*e* **1/3 marks awarded.** This is another example of failing to read the question. There are 3 marks available here and all Student B has done is to identify an alternative technique. To achieve more marks you would need to explain how a random sample might have been generated in this study (for example, by using the sixth form register and a random number generator).

> **5 (a)** Scales are really easy for participants to complete.

*e* **0/2 marks awarded.** This is a very short answer and does not tell the examiner much. 'Easy' needs to be explained a little further. Why is this easy and even more importantly why is 'easy' a strength? There is the beginning of an appropriate answer here but the examiner would not award any credit for this without further elaboration.

> **(b)** One problem is the scale that has been used. It may be that different people understand different things by the phrases 'not important' and 'extremely important', which means it could be difficult to analyse the results.

*e* **2/2 marks awarded.** This is a good answer. This is a very precise and well explained point.

> **6** This would be in the discussion.

*e* **1/1 mark awarded.** This is correct. A consideration of future research would be included in the discussion.

> **7** I would do this study again but with older people.

*e* **1/4 marks awarded.** This is another very short answer which would gain a maximum of 1 mark out of a possible 4. It is really important that you check how many marks there are for each question and use this to guide your answer. Student B needed to expand on this basic idea and give more detail. How much older? How many people? Where would they come from? Why is this a good idea for some future research? All of this is fairly straightforward if you spend a minute or two thinking about your answer before you write.

*e* **Total score: 13/25 marks. This could easily have been improved if Student B had spent a little more time on each answer and ensured that the answers were explained fully.**

# A-level example 1

Total: 35 marks

A psychology teacher wishes to see if there is a correlation between her students' liking for psychology and the score they achieve on a classroom test. She asks them to rate their enjoyment of psychology on a 1–10 scale where 1 is 'I don't enjoy psychology at all' and 10 is 'I enjoy psychology more than any other subject I have studied'. She then gave her students a multiple-choice test with 20 questions covering the material they had been studying over the past few weeks. The results are shown in the table.

| Participant | Enjoyment of psychology self-rating | Score on a 20 question multiple-choice test |
|---|---|---|
| 1 | 10 | 18 |
| 2 | 10 | 20 |
| 3 | 8 | 19 |
| 4 | 8 | 15 |
| 5 | 8 | 16 |
| 6 | 7 | 13 |
| 7 | 5 | 10 |
| 8 | 5 | 12 |
| 9 | 4 | 2 |
| 10 | 1 | 0 |

**1** Suggest an appropriate hypothesis for this study. (4 marks)

ⓔ You are asked for an appropriate hypothesis for this study. The study is correlational, so writing a hypothesis for an experiment will not gain you any marks. A hypothesis that says something like 'there will be a correlation between the scores' will be awarded 1 mark. Including both the variables clearly within the hypothesis will gain 2–3 marks. 4 marks will be awarded to a hypothesis that includes all the relevant information and is clearly and appropriately worded.

**2** Explain why a correlation is an appropriate technique to use to investigate this hypothesis. (5 marks)

ⓔ The first thing to notice about this question is that there are 5 marks available. This should tell you that you will need to write a few sentences for your answer and give a full explanation. The examiner will be looking for an understanding of correlation as a technique for calculating the strength of a relationship between two variables which is what is required here. There is no manipulation of an independent variable here which would require the use of an experimental method. Here the researcher has simply measured two variables (enjoyment and score on a test) and is looking to see what the relationship between them is.

**3** From the data in the table:
  **(a)** What is the modal score for enjoyment of psychology? (1 mark)
  **(b)** What is the median result for the multiple-choice test? (1 mark)
  **(c)** What is the mean score for the enjoyment of psychology? (1 mark)

**e** For each part of this question there is simply 1 mark for the correct answer. You should be able to work each of these out easily enough but remember that you are allowed to use a calculator in this exam, so if the calculation for the mean is too difficult to work out in your head you can always use your calculator.

**4    Sketch a scatter graph of the data given in the table.**    (4 marks)

**e** If you simply plot the points without scales or labels, you will be awarded 1 mark. A graph with some labelling but significant omissions will be awarded 2 marks, and one with only minor omissions will be awarded 3 marks. A graph that has been fully and clearly labelled will gain the full 4 marks. Remember that you are just being asked to 'sketch' the graph, so there are no marks for accuracy of scale.

**5    (a)  Suggest one problem with the measurement of enjoyment and one problem with the measurement of achievement.**    (4 marks)

**e** This question asks for two problems and there are 2 marks for each problem. The examiner will award 1 mark if you simply identify a problem and another mark if you describe the problem clearly or give some additional information such as explaining why something is a problem.

**(b)  Describe and evaluate an alternative way of measuring one of these variables.**    (6 marks)

**e** This question asks you to describe an alternative way of measuring one of the variables and to evaluate this. There will be 3 marks for your description and 3 marks for your evaluation. For the description, simply identifying an alternative (e.g. 'observation') will get you 1 mark, but you will need increasing detail about exactly how you are going to measure the variable to achieve further marks. For 3 marks, it is worth trying to identify and explain (in context) one strength and one weakness of your suggestion. Identifying strengths and weaknesses will get you 1 mark, explaining or discussing them a little more will get you 2 marks and discussing them in the context of this study will get you the third mark.

**6    (a)  The psychologist analysed the data using the Spearman's rho test. Give two reasons for this choice of test with reference to the study.**    (4 marks)

**e** The key part of this question is the requirement to make 'reference to the study'. Rather than just giving single word or phrases for each reason you need to make sure that you show how this is relevant to this piece of research. The reasons for using a Spearman's rho test would be that you were looking for a correlation (as opposed to a difference) and that the data were ordinal (or non-parametric).

**(b)  The Spearman's rho gave an observed (calculated) value of 0.95.**

| Levels of significance for a one-tailed test significance level | 0.05 | 0.025 | 0.01 |
|---|---|---|---|
| Critical value | 0.648 | 0.745 | 0.794 |

**Using the above critical values, explain whether the psychologist has found a significant correlation.**    (4 marks)

ⓔ You should be familiar with these tables and be able to interpret whether a calculated value means that you have reached a level of significance sufficient to accept your hypothesis and reject your null hypothesis. Ideally you should explain this process (compare calculated to critical value) and also make reference to the probability levels as well as the final conclusions in relation to the hypothesis that can be drawn. There are 4 marks for this question so make sure you include enough to earn all 4 marks.

**7    Where would this information be placed in the final written report?**    (1 mark)

ⓔ There is 1 mark available here and the answer is that this would be in the results section. This is all you need to say for 1 mark.

> **Student A**
>
> **1**    There will be a significant positive correlation between the rating of enjoyment a student gives to A-level psychology and the score they achieve on a multiple-choice psychology test.

ⓔ **4/4 marks awarded.** This is a clear correlational hypothesis, for full marks.

**2**    This is a correlation because the researcher is looking for a correlation between the students' enjoyment of psychology and how well they did on a test.

ⓔ **0/5 marks awarded.** This will not achieve any marks as the answer does no more than copy out the first sentence of the information given on the exam paper. This is a shame as had Student A explained this a little more, perhaps by using the word 'relationship' rather than correlation this would have at least been worth 1 mark. Obviously, when a question is worth 5 marks you need to give more than a sentence. Student A needed to go on to explain the lack of manipulation of variables in a correlation rather than an experiment and the fact that this is an appropriate way to investigate variables such as these.

> **3    (a)** The modal score is 8.

ⓔ **1/1 mark awarded.** This is correct. The modal score is the most popular score.

> **(b)** The median score is 14.

ⓔ **1/1 mark awarded.** This is also correct.

> **(c)** The mean is 6.6

ⓔ **1/1 mark awarded.** This is the correct answer.

**4**

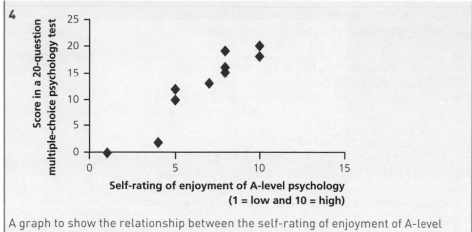

A graph to show the relationship between the self-rating of enjoyment of A-level psychology and a score in a 20-question multiple-choice test

**ℯ 4/4 marks awarded.** The student has labelled the axes clearly and the scatter graph is easy to understand.

**5 (a)** One problem with the measure of enjoyment is that participants might respond to demand characteristics, especially if the psychology teacher asked them the question. Some students might have felt that they had to say that they liked psychology and some may have exaggerated their lack of enjoyment because they don't like the teacher or are not doing well. Enjoyment is also measured on a scale and different people might respond to the scale differently. One problem with the multiple-choice test is that people might get some answers right just by guessing. If there were four choices for each answer, people might get the right one about 25% of the time, which in a set of 20 questions could make a huge difference. Therefore, this might not be a valid way of measuring achievement.

**ℯ 4/4 marks awarded.** This is an excellent answer. The student has suggested an appropriate problem with both measures and these have been explained well for full marks.

**(b)** A good alternative for the multiple-choice test might be to give the students a different type of test. This test could be short answers but there would be no multiple choice. It would be less likely that students would get the right answer by chance.

**ℯ 3/6 marks awarded.** This answer requires more detail. An appropriate alternative has been given — we know that the new test would include short answers and not multiple-choice questions, but we do not know anything else. The evaluation is brief and the answer gains only 3 marks.

**6 (a)** The researcher would have selected the Spearman's rho test because she was looking for a correlation and because the data were ordinal.

**e 2/4 marks awarded.** Although both the answers given are correct there is no link between these reasons and the study being discussed here. Student A needed to explain a little more about the correlation and why the data are best seen as ordinal.

**(b)** Yes it is significant because the calculated value is bigger than the critical value and this means that it is significant.

**e 1/4 marks awarded.** This is correct but there were 4 marks available for this and this is only enough to achieve 1 mark. Student A needed to go further than this and explain the appropriate probability level and what this means and also say whether the researcher could then accept her hypothesis and reject the null hypothesis.

**7** Results.

**e 1/1 mark awarded.** This is correct.

**e Total score: 22/35 marks. There is a real mix of excellent answers with ones that failed to achieve any marks at all.**

**Student B**

**1** Enjoyment will affect test scores.

**e 0/4 marks awarded.** This is not a correlational hypothesis and gains no marks. A correlational hypothesis should state that there is a relationship between the two variables, not that one variable will affect the other.

**2** The researcher has chosen a correlation to investigate whether enjoyment will affect test scores.

**e 0/5 marks awarded.** This is incorrect. Student B has carried forward her mistake from question 1 and is not demonstrating any understanding of a correlation.

**3 (a)** The mode is 6.6.

**e 0/1 mark awarded.** This is incorrect. The figure the student has given is the mean rather than the mode.

**(b)** The median is 13 and 16.

e **0/1 mark awarded.** Again, this is incorrect. The median is the mid-point between these two scores (14.5). To calculate a median, you put the scores in rank order and then find the mid-point. If this is between two scores (as it will be in a set of 10), you have to work out the mid-point of those two.

> **(c)** The mean is 66.

e **0/1 mark awarded.** This is another incorrect answer. Unfortunately Student B has just missed the final step of the calculation. This is the total of the enjoyment scores. What still needs to be done is to divide this number by 10 (the number of scores) which would have given a mean of 6.6.

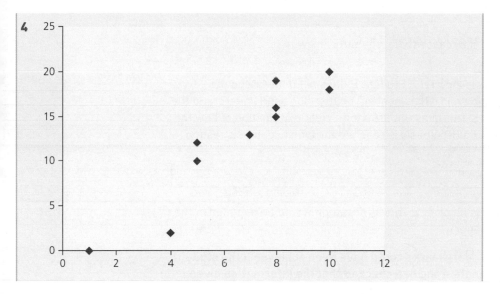

e **1/4 marks awarded.** This scatter graph has been plotted correctly but the student has not included any labelling. Therefore, the graph does not tell us anything and is only awarded 1 mark.

> **5 (a)** One problem with the measurement of enjoyment is that people might lie. One problem with the multiple-choice test is that people might cheat.

e **2/4 marks awarded.** Only brief answers are given here. The first problem identified is worth 1 mark as this is true, people might lie. However, there needs to be more information explaining why they might lie in this particular investigation. The second point is a weak one. People might cheat in all kinds of tests but are they any more likely to cheat in a multiple-choice test? A generous interpretation accepts this answer as appropriate and 1 mark is awarded.

> **(b)** An alternative to the rating of enjoyment might be to ask students to guess how many answers they might get right.

**ⓔ 0/6 marks awarded.** The student has not read the question properly. Although this is an interesting suggestion for another variable that could be investigated, it does not answer the question, which asks for an alternative way of measuring one of the variables rather than an alternative variable that could be measured. This is not an alternative way of measuring enjoyment, so no marks are awarded.

> **6** **(a)** Spearman's rho tells you if there is a significant difference.

**ⓔ 0/4 marks awarded.** This is incorrect. Spearman's rho tests for a correlation (or a relationship) rather than a difference. It is also necessary to explain that some tests are appropriate for some types of data. Spearman's rho is used when data are ordinal rather than interval.

> **(b)** No, there is no effect because the probability is low.

**ⓔ 0/4 marks awarded.** This is incorrect. Student B does not understand the difference between correlation and difference and neither does she understand the process of hypothesis testing. This question asks for a clear explanation of how the final decision to accept/reject a hypothesis is reached through hypothesis testing.

> **7** At the end.

**ⓔ 0/1 mark awarded.** This is incorrect. This information would be included in the results section of the final report.

**ⓔ Total score: 3/35 marks. More marks could have been achieved if the student had provided greater explanation and had checked that the information given was what was asked for in the question. These answers demonstrate the importance of thinking carefully before starting to write.**

# A-level example 2

Total: 35 marks

A researcher has conducted an observation of mobile phone usage. He sat in a café working on his laptop and every so often he stopped working and looked out of the window. He observed the first 200 men and the first 200 women that walked past him in a shopping centre on a weekday lunchtime. He recorded whether they were using a mobile phone and if they were, whether they were talking or texting. His results are shown in the table.

| | Male | Female |
|---|---|---|
| No. of people using mobile phones (out of 200) | 33 | 78 |
| No. of people not using mobile phones (out of 200) | 167 | 122 |
| No. of people talking on mobile phones (out of 33 and 78 respectively) | 26 | 67 |
| No. of people texting on mobile phones (out of 33 and 78 respectively) | 7 | 11 |

**1** Outline two conclusions that can be drawn from the results. (4 marks)

ⓔ You are simply asked for two conclusions, with 2 marks for each.

**2 (a)** What kind of sampling method did the researcher use? (2 marks)

ⓔ 1 mark will be awarded for an answer that lacks clarity and 2 marks will be given for a clear and accurate answer.

**(b)** Outline one strength and one weakness of using this sampling method for this observation. (6 marks)

ⓔ 3 marks are available for outlining a strength and 3 marks for a weakness. Simply identifying a general strength or weakness would be enough for 1 mark, elaborating on this would get the second mark, and giving an answer which clearly explained the strength or weakness in the context of this observation would achieve 3 marks.

**3** Describe and evaluate two changes that could be made to this observation. (10 marks)

ⓔ This question asks you to describe and evaluate and there are 5 marks for each part. You will need to describe two changes — just identifying possible changes or giving a brief suggestion would get no more than 2 marks. Further marks will be awarded for increasing detail (the question says 'describe' rather than 'identify' or 'outline'), and 5 marks would be awarded for an answer that described two possible changes clearly. For the evaluation, just identifying a strength or weakness or the possible effects of these changes would get you no more than 2 marks. Discussing these points in more detail and in the context of this observation will be expected for more marks. 5 marks will be awarded for an answer that clearly discusses the implications of the changes on the observation.

**4** The researcher used a Chi-squared test to analyse the results. Give two reasons why this is the appropriate test to use for this investigation. (4 marks)

ⓔ This question could be asked about any of the tests. You need to know which test is used for which type of data and for which type of research question. Chi-squared tests are used to analyse nominal data when the researcher is looking for an association.

**5** Explain how the researcher will conclude whether the calculated value of Chi-squared means that there was a significant difference between the way men and women used their phones. (4 marks)

ⓔ Calculating a score from a formula is only half the story. Once you have your calculated value you need to look this up in a significance table and this will tell you the probability of the result being due to chance. The smaller the probability that the result is due to chance the more secure you can be in accepting the hypothesis and rejecting the null hypothesis. No one is going to expect you to know the critical values from the significance table and this question is only asking for a description of this process.

**6** Describe the process of peer review. (2 marks)

ⓔ Peer review is when articles that have been submitted for publication in academic journals are sent to other academics working in similar areas to review.

**7**  Outline one limitation of the process of peer review.  (3 marks)

ⓔ It should be obvious that this process is not without its problems. One of the main criticisms of this process is that it simply does not work as there are examples of poor research that has been published despite having been through this process. It is also a very time consuming and slow process which means that research may not be published very quickly. Finally, some areas of research are relatively small and all the people working in that area probably know each other and know what other researchers are working on. This means that the anonymity is probably not that successful as the peer reviewer will know (or guess) who has written the article. If they see them as rivals or disagree with their approach this might make them less than objective when judging the work.

---

**Student A**

**1**  In the shopping centre at lunchtime, only 33 men out of 200 observed were using their phones, whereas 78 women out of 200 were. This would strongly suggest that females use their phones more frequently than men. The second conclusion would be that using a mobile phone for talking is more popular than texting, as nearly four times as many people were talking on phones than texting.

ⓔ **4/4 marks awarded.** These are conclusions (rather than just results) and 2 marks are awarded for each conclusion.

**2**  **(a)** This is an opportunity sample as the researcher simply observed the first 200 men and women who walked past him at the time and place he was conducting his study.

ⓔ **2/2 marks awarded.** This answer gets full marks as it identifies the correct sampling method and explains this.

**(b)** Opportunity sampling is quick and easy as the researcher can simply take advantage of the sample that is there at the time they want it. They do not have to go through a lengthy selection procedure. Assuming that the researcher did not want a specific age or other characteristic, the advantages of the sampling method probably outweigh the disadvantages. The disadvantage of an opportunity sampling method is that it does not produce a representative sample as all the people were all in the same place at the same time. For example, in this study this would exclude everyone who was not in the shopping centre and might give a skewed sample in terms of age, gender and occupation.

ⓔ **6/6 marks awarded.** This is a clear answer that explains a strength and a weakness and relates them to the observation. Although there could have been more detail, there is enough here for full marks.

**3** I would change the position of the observer. This observation is really looking at people who are using their mobile phones and walking round the shopping centre at the same time. Maybe more people stop to answer their phones or to make a call or a text. Perhaps observing people in the shopping centre's largest eating area or seating area would allow you to see more people using phones. This would give me a lot more data to analyse. I would also record the approximate age of everyone that was observed so that I could analyse the results in more detail. This would perhaps show that older people are less likely to be using their phones than younger people.

🅮 **7/10 marks awarded.** The student has given two appropriate changes and explained them. There is some evaluation, but for a 10-mark question the examiner is looking for more. Note that the question asks for changes rather than improvements, and this means, for example, that you could identify a strength and a weakness for each of your suggestions. This answer is awarded 4 marks for the suggestions and 3 marks for the evaluation.

**4** A Chi-squared test is designed to look for the difference between the expected frequencies of data and the actual frequencies of data when the data are nominal. This means that we might expect that there would be no difference between the numbers of men and the numbers of women using phones and so the test compares the actual frequencies with what would be expected by chance. Nominal data means that the data are in categories as these data are here (using phone or not using phone).

🅮 **4/4 marks awarded.** This is a very clear answer to the question and demonstrates excellent understanding.

**5** The Chi-squared test gives you a calculated value which then needs to be looked up in a significance table. If the calculated value is larger than the critical value then the probability of the results being due to chance is low enough to accept the hypothesis and reject the null hypothesis (that the results are due to chance).

🅮 **3/4 marks awarded.** This is a very good answer which would achieve at least 3 marks out of 4. A brief mention of the p values might add to the detail.

**6** The process of peer review is that researchers submit their articles for publication in academic journals. The editors of the journal send the article (anonymised) to a number of other academic researchers working in similar areas and they comment on the validity of the research and raise any questions or concerns they might have. The original author may have to make changes to their article as a result of these comments.

🅮 **2/2 marks awarded.** There is plenty here for full marks. This is a good description of the process of peer review.

> **7** The process is not always fair as a reviewer might not want the article published if it contradicts their work or if it is better than their work.

🅔 **2/3 marks awarded.** This response is worth 2 marks, 1 for identifying that the process may not always be fair and another for the elaboration, but this answer could have been much clearer and more detailed.

🅔 **Total score: 30/35 marks. There are some very detailed and well explained responses here.**

> **Student B**
>
> **1** 33 men were using mobile phones. 26 were talking and 7 were texting.

🅔 **0/4 marks awarded.** These are not conclusions and gain no marks. The answer goes no further than repeating the information that has been given in the tables.

> **2 (a)** An opportunity sample.

🅔 **1/2 marks awarded.** The sampling method is an opportunity sample, but the examiner is expecting a little more for 2 marks. The student could have explained why this is an opportunity sample to ensure the second mark.

> **(b)** Opportunity sampling is quick and easy. Not representative.

🅔 **2/6 marks awarded.** The examiner definitely expects more here. The strength and weakness identified are correct and achieve 1 mark each, but both are brief and lack detail. Neither has been given in the context of the specific observation being discussed.

> **3** Use more participants and observe in a different place.

🅔 **2/10 marks awarded.** Once again, two valid changes have been identified for 1 mark each, but the answer is brief and vague and the changes have not been evaluated.

> **4** Because the data are nominal.

🅔 **1/4 marks awarded.** The question asks for two reasons and more information would be required for this to get 4 marks.

> **5** The researcher needs to look this up in the table.

**e** **1/4 marks awarded.** Student B is correct to say that there is a table involved, but what table is this and what needs to be looked up? A better answer would be to explain that the Chi-squared test produces a calculated value which needs to be looked up in a significance table. If the value of Chi-squared is larger than the number in the table then the difference between male and female use of mobile phones is significant and the null hypothesis can be rejected. If not then the null hypothesis must be retained.

> **6** Peer review is a check to make sure that the research is good enough to be published.

**e** **1/2 marks awarded.** Student B is correct to say that peer review checks the research before it is published but there is a little more to it than that. It is important to include an explanation of the term 'peer' in this. Papers are sent to academics working in similar areas (peers) and they are asked to review the paper before its inclusion in the journal.

> **7** The reviewer might be biased as he doesn't want anyone else to publish on this topic.

**e** **1/3 marks awarded.** This is a reasonable point, but the examiners will be looking for a lot more information that this for 3 marks.

**e** **Total score: 9/35 marks. Student B has missed lots of opportunities to give more detail or more explanation.**

# Answers to multiple-choice questions

## AS questions

| | | | | | | | | | |
|---|---|---|---|---|---|---|---|---|---|
| 1 | B. | 4 | A. | 7 | A. | 10 | D. | 13 | C. |
| 2 | C. | 5 | B. | 8 | D. | 11 | B. | 14 | A. |
| 3 | C. | 6 | B. | 9 | B. | 12 | C. | 15 | D. |

## A-level questions

| | | | | | | | | | |
|---|---|---|---|---|---|---|---|---|---|
| 1 | C. | 5 | B. | 9 | D. | 13 | C. | 17 | D. |
| 2 | A. | 6 | C. | 10 | C. | 14 | B. | 18 | B. |
| 3 | C. | 7 | A. | 11 | B. | 15 | A. | 19 | A. |
| 4 | C. | 8 | A. | 12 | C. | 16 | D. | 20 | C. |

# Knowledge check answers

**Knowledge check answers**

1 The study by Piliavin was conducted in a natural environment but is still an experiment because the independent variable was manipulated. The strengths of this method include (a) high ecological validity and (b) low demand characteristics because participants do not know they are being studied. The weaknesses include (a) a lack of control over the situation and (b) ethical problems, as people have not given their consent to be part of an experiment and may also be distressed by what occurred.

2 A covert observation is one that is conducted without the participants' knowledge. The strengths of this include a lack of demand characteristics as people are unaware that they are being observed. This also means that the behaviour observed will be natural. However, this may be a highly unethical technique. While observing without people's knowledge may be acceptable in certain situations (e.g. observing which way people walk around shops), this will not always be the case. Observing people in hospitals or at work may be perceived very differently. An overt observation is one in which people know that they are being observed. This removes the ethical problems but increases the likelihood of demand characteristics.

3 Bandura used observational techniques to code the behaviour of the children in the final part of his experiment. The study by Rosenhan (A-level) used participant observation with the pseudo-patients acting as the observers.

4 Strengths of self-report methods include: the fact that you are asking people directly; that you can gain large amounts of data relatively easily (especially with questionnaires); that they are easy to replicate and if questions are open, you can gain a great deal of insight. Weaknesses include: social desirability bias; forcing people to choose from a selection of answers that may not represent their opinion; difficulty in producing questions that are free from bias; and the difficulties associated with analysing open questions.

5 Weaknesses might be the individual experience/ skill/enjoyment of each person doing jigsaw puzzles. Alternative ways are probably endless but could include a task that involves sorting things into groups, crossing a particular letter out of a passage of writing, building a model and so on.

6 The answer is C. The explanation is that you have only demonstrated that there is a relationship between the two and not that there is any cause and effect. Of course, either A or B (or both) could be true, but you would have to test this experimentally before you could draw a cause and effect conclusion.

7 The target population was males between 20 and 50 years of age living in the New Haven area. They were recruited through newspaper and direct mail advertisements. The sample was the 40 males who took part in the experiment.

8 You would have to consider whether students who use the quiet study room at lunchtime are typical (representative) of all students in the target population. For the second study, you would have to consider whether volunteers are typical (representative) of the general population. Is it possible that they might be more helpful than the general population? (They did volunteer after all!)

9 The independent variable is the lighting. There are two conditions of this variable: a poorly-lit room and a well-lit room.

10 **Strengths** include:
- the lack of order effects (participants would not get better/worse because they are only doing the task once)
- low demand characteristics (participants are unlikely to figure out what is being tested because they are only doing the task once)
- you could use the same task in each condition (because there are different people in each condition)

**Weaknesses** include:
- individual differences (people in one group might be naturally better at the task than the people in the other group)
- you would need twice as many participants as you would need for a repeated measures design

11 **Strengths** include:
- individual differences are not an issue, as you have the same people in each condition
- you would only need half as many people as you would need for an independent measures design

**Weaknesses** include:
- there is a higher chance of order effects and demand characteristics
- you would probably need a different task in each condition, which could cause further problems if the tasks were not equivalent

12 There are obviously many possible answers to this, but your answer should define exactly what you mean by 'naughtiness' and perhaps consider issues such as the number of naughty acts or the severity of these acts. By defining exactly what you mean, you will be able to measure your variable more precisely.

13 Perhaps some of the participants had more driving experience than others. This might mean that they were more confident in their estimate of speed and hence less likely to be influenced by a 'leading' word in the question. Perhaps some had been in an accident themselves, or been a witness to an accident, and the emotional associations may have produced a confounding variable.

14 Mainly because low inter-rater reliability is a source of bias. In the same way that it should be possible to replicate an experiment, it should be possible to replicate an observation. The observational categories (or schedule) should be able to be used by multiple observers in exactly the same way. The results should not be affected by the person doing the observing.

**15** ■ Observer ratings of attractiveness is ORDINAL
   ■ Number of people answering yes in a referendum is NOMINAL
   ■ Number of errors in a proof reading task is probably INTERVAL (provided we can be sure that all the errors are equally easy/difficult to spot, if we are not sure about this we would be better treating these data as ORDINAL)
   ■ IQ scores are best treated as ORDINAL — even though these might look like interval data, we cannot be sure that all the questions are equally easy/difficult and so we cannot be sure that the intervals between the scores are consistent
   ■ Time taken to sort a pack of cards is INTERVAL — we know that a scale of measurement in seconds has the same interval between each point on the scale

**16** A way to measure driving skill using nominal data would be the number of people who finished a driving task and the number of people who failed to finish. A way to measure driving skill using ordinal data would be who came first, second, third and so on. Finally, a way to measure driving skill using interval data would be the actual times it took people to complete the task.

**17** ■ Repeated measures and ordinal level data — Wilcoxon sign test
   ■ Correlation and interval level (parametric) data — Pearson's product moment
   ■ Repeated measures and interval level (parametric) data — related t-test
   ■ Independent measures and nominal data — Chi-squared test
   ■ Independent measures and interval level (parametric) data — unrelated t-test
   ■ Correlation and ordinal level data — Spearman's rho
   ■ Independent measures and ordinal level data — Mann–Whitney U-test

**18** There are lots of possible answers that you could give here. Milgram's sample was all males so may not generalise to females, Sperry's sample was a very small number of people who had severe epilepsy so may not generalise to a group of people without epilepsy, Freud's sample was just one small

boy and so on. In fact it might be useful to consider whether you can identify a study in which you can generalise easily from the sample that was selected.

**19** The simple answer is that they are probably not valid at all. However, this does not seem to stop us enjoying filling them in and getting an answer. It is unlikely that they have been subjected to any of the checks on validity that would be used for psychological tests.

**20** You have probably said 'no' to Bandura and 'yes' to Piliavin. Bandura's study was conducted in an artificial and unfamiliar environment, which is likely to mean that any behaviour displayed is not necessarily the same as that displayed in the participants 'normal' environment. Piliavin's study was conducted in a natural environment and as it was highly unlikely that the participants knew they were being studied, their behaviour was likely to be natural.

**21** There are many possible examples here. Do you think that the participants in Milgram's study may have acted in the way they did in order to please the experimenter? Do you think Little Hans may have answered some questions to please his father?

**22** Again there are many possible answers here. If you chose the behaviour of the experimenter in the study by Milgram you could consider how changes to this behaviour affect the level of obedience shown.

**23** This one is up to you. Students often choose Milgram when asked to pick the most unethical and it is easy to see why. However, the study by Bandura also raises some ethical issues which could perhaps be seen as more serious as the study involved children.

**24** This one is up to you. Do any of the studies you have covered in your course raise no ethical issues at all?

**25** Plagiarism is when we attempt to pass someone else's work off as our own. This might include behaviours such as copying a whole essay from someone else (or from the internet) or failing to acknowledge (using a citation and a reference) that the arguments you are presenting came from something you have read. Plagiarism is really important when you are a higher education student as passing someone else's work off as your own would be seen as academic misconduct.

# Index

Note: locators for definitions appear in **bold**. Locators for diagrams appear in *italic*.

# Index